Meaning In Myth:
Three Separate Journeys

Thomas M. Casey, OSA

Sheed & Ward

Sheed & Ward™ is a service of National Catholic Reporter Publishing
Company, Inc.

Library of Congress Catalog Card Number: 89-61931

ISBN: 1-55612-253-5

Published by: Sheed & Ward
              115 E. Armour Blvd. P.O. Box 419492
              Kansas City, MO 64141-6492

To order, call: (800) 333-7373

Contents

Preface v

1. Reality and Meaning: The Search for Both 1

2. Religion and Science: The Truth of the Myth 9

3. Atheism and Agnosticism: Alternative Myths 18

4. Experience: The Basis of Myth 31

5. The Critical Analysis of Myths 42

6. Three Universal Religious Myths 59

7. The Buddha: The Myth of the Search 65

8. The Christ: The Myth of the Person 80

9. Muhammed: The Myth of the Book 100

10. Concluding Remarks 115

Notes 121

Preface

An incredible volume of material exists that deals with religious experience and behavior, attitudes and values, *etc.* Phenomenologists,* sociologists, psychologists, economists, political pundits, theologians, and the average person all have ideas about religion and its meaning. The very attempt to define religion is problematic and gives rise to as many objections as agreements. Religion is social and yet intensely personal, as Gordon Allport observed:

> The conclusion that we come to is that the subjective religious attitude of every individual is, in both its essential and nonessential features unlike that of any other individual. The roots of religion are so numerous, the weight of their influence so varied, and the forms of rational interpretation so endless that uniformity of product is impossible. Only in respect to certain basic biological functions do men closely resemble one another. In the higher reaches of personality uniqueness of organization becomes more apparent and since no department of personality is subject to more complex development than the religious sentiment, it is precisely in this area that we must expect to find the ultimate divergence.[1]

It is rather meaningless to talk of "religion" as though it were a single empirical entity or a ubiquitous personal experience had by many persons in the same way. I think it useful to deal with religious experience in a phenomenological manner, letting the experience "speak for itself" and, later in our study, investigating some major religious experiences as seen in the lives and teachings of great religious figures. The central roles of the Buddha, the Christ and of Muhammed will, when sympathetically under-

* See glossary at end of chapter.

stood, enable us to better appreciate the human condition and the questions that all reflective individuals ask about life, its purpose and goal.

This book is an invitation to a journey wherein we shall seek to learn what religion has to say about human needs, desires, fears, hopes and ideals. There will be no attempt made to present simple answers but rather to raise questions and to move the student beyond parochial assumptions. In brief, I hope to expose the student to ideas and viewpoints that will challenge his or her certitude about "the way things are." Education is an evolutionary process that should continue throughout our lives and serve to make us curious about the world around and within us. Religion serves many functions for individuals, as Allport noted, but perhaps the most important one is that of making sense of our place and purpose in the universe. One's personal religious convictions—or lack of them—are a private matter, but the study of religion transcends the individual and speaks to concerns common to all persons.

The functionalist school of sociology judges that when something ceases to have a function it ceases to exist. The existence of religion throughout the ages testifies to its central role in human self-knowledge. To be ignorant of religion or simplistic in evaluating its complex nature is really to have less understanding of ourselves. The study of religion is a vital guidepost along the life-long journey into self-discovery.

Glossary

Phenomenology is a branch of philosophy that avoids judging the objective reality or the subjective response to a phenomenon. It is only concerned with describing and observing what it investigates.

1.

Reality and Meaning: The Search for Both

Sigmund Freud (1856-1939), in a letter to Marie Bonaparte, August 13, 1937, stated: "The moment one inquires about the sense or value of life, one is sick, since objectively neither of them has any existence."[2] Freud, the gifted father of psychoanalysis, was suffering greatly from cancer of the jaw at this point in his life. In less than two years he would be dead, and perhaps we might reasonably surmise that Freud's dark thoughts were filtered through a curtain of anger and bitterness. The intensity of his statement is noteworthy but it actually is consistent with his life-long conviction, shared by many of his contemporaries, that there is no meaning in the universe beyond that which we happen to give it. There is no absolute, no structure of meaning, no plan that exists outside of us. Meaning, if any, is created not discovered.

An older generation of moviegoers wistfully talk of movies that had a "happy ending" and that had a plot that allowed the viewer to make a clear moral judgment. No longer is this the case. Increasingly our plays, films and novels reflect Freud's conviction that life is too complex for neat patterns of meaning to be found.

Another famous Jew, Albert Einstein, often mistakenly viewed as an atheist, had a totally different understanding of reality: "My religion consists of a humble admiration of the illimitable superior spirit who reveals himself in the slight details we are able to perceive with our frail and feeble minds. That deeply emotional conviction of the presence of a supe-

1

rior reasoning power, which is revealed in the incomprehensible universe, forms my idea of God."[3] Here Einstein clearly perceives a purpose and a plan in the universe which we can only partially comprehend.

How does it happen that two brilliant thinkers can reach such diametrically opposed viewpoints? The answer is complex but explanations have been attempted by psychologists, sociologists, philosophers and theologians. Let us briefly consider how we come to "know" what is "real."

Psychology talks of a bimodal human brain, the left hemisphere controlling language, rational cognition and a time sense, the right hemisphere emphasizing intuition, spatial relationships and creativity. Some persons tend, by training or temperament, to be left-hemisphere or right-hemisphere persons almost exclusively. Thus some persons are most distrustful of feelings, whereas others are impatient with logical analysis.[4]

The niece of a friend of mine related her experience of dating three different engineering students from a prestigious Boston university. She complained that they had no interest in museums, theater, novels, music, *etc.*, and that she did not wish to discuss bridges and highways on a date. Needless to say, they soon parted company.

Einstein notes, from a right-hemisphere perspective:

myth def.

> The most beautiful and most profound emotion we can experience is the sensation of the mystical. It is the sower of all true science. He to whom this emotion is a stranger, who can no longer wonder and stand rapt in awe, is as good as dead. To know that what is impenetrable to us really exists, manifesting itself as the highest wisdom and the most radiant beauty which our dull faculties can comprehend only in their most primitive forms— this knowledge, this feeling is at the center of true religiousness.[5]

Some, perhaps many, persons seem incapable of such awe, reverie or emotion. Freud claimed never to have had a religious experience, although he never hesitated to interpret the religious experiences described by others, much as a person who had never dreamed would create a theory of dream interpretation.[6]

What kind of person is capable of moving comfortably and safely between the world of social reality and that of private reverie? One psychologist suggests that it is those adults who, as children, were encouraged by their parents to indulge their fantasies and imagination. They were allowed to explore their own inner spaces and were guided by their parents in returning to established social norms:

> This background gives the temperament capable of deep religious experiences, empathy, compassion, ability to see from a different world view, willingness to agree quickly with the adversary, and other marks of a flexible tolerance that does not feel threatened by strangeness.[7]

It seems that only an individual who is open to various dimensions of reality is truly capable of religious experience. Freud believed that religion was dangerous because it impoverished intelligence by making critical reasoning suspect. Although he did not employ the term, Freud was a left-hemisphere thinker who believed reality was exclusively structured by reason and empirical demonstration. We shall return to Freud later, because he made some valid criticisms of religion, in spite of his sweeping generalizations.

Philosophers prefer to talk of epistemologies, that is, systems of knowledge employed to deal with reality. There are basically four epistemologies corresponding to the bimodal model of the human brain favored by the psychologist. These are: rationalism (thinking), empiricism (sensory verification), intuition (feeling) and authoritarianism (believing).[8] Each epistemology has a primary criterion for truth and a clear procedure for judging truth or falsity. Science favors rationalism and empiricism; philosophy, rationalism; art, intuition; and religion, rationalism and intuition.

Each epistemology serves a different, if sometimes complementary, purpose and is *one* approach to reality. To employ the same epistemology in all circumstances may be inadequate or irrelevant.

Because the logic of maps escapes me—something to do, I suspect, with a disastrous introduction to plane geometry in high school—I intuit my destination, usually arriving late after driving around aimlessly. Likewise a very rational person may disconcert an artist by asking "what it means" rather than just being "present" to the creative work.

Many creative scientists are intuitive in their approach to problem-solving just as some artists are very logical in their techniques, so we should be cautious in aligning various disciplines and epistemologies. The point to be made is that one epistemology is not "better" than another, just as one hemisphere of the brain is not "superior" to the other. Reality is much too complex and multifaceted to be contained within any limited paradigm.[9]

Authoritarianism is the epistemology employed by the individual afraid to think for oneself. It is a temptation from which no one is fully immune and which may subtly color our perceptions in ways we are not conscious of. Some persons would vote for a total incompetent if he were nominated by their political party. Within religion this mind-set is exemplified by a bumper sticker I saw recently that said: "God revealed it. I believe it. That's the end of it." In another instance, I remember a graduate student relating his experience in Europe studying under a disciple of a great psychologist. Whenever a student asked a question the professor would inevitably open the collected works of the psychologist and respond: "Let us see what the Master has to say."

The point of this brief discussion is to make the student aware that each epistemology, or system of knowledge, seeks to know what is "real" or "true" from its own perspective but that no one approach exhausts "reality." It is only when an individual or group adopts authoritarianism that the death of the mind and the beginning of smug intolerance of other viewpoints ensue.

Darwin lamented late in his life that the demands of his scientific enterprise had led gradually to a loss of appreciation for art and music, to an underdevelopment of the emotions, a process he believed was possibly injurious to his intellect. Darwin was obviously not demeaning science but rather acknowledging that the world of "facts" is only a partial reality. Likewise, the humanist who ignores the natural sciences is as myopic and encapsulated as the narrow specialist who never considers what his "facts" really "mean" in an ultimate sense. We shall expand on these ideas when we explore the so-called conflict between religion and science.

Another discipline which gives us some insight into the way that we structure reality is the sociology of knowledge, a special focus within a larger area of study. These sociologists study the processes by which human knowledge is developed, transmitted and maintained in social situations. It is common for them to speak of the "social construction" of "reality"[10] and to analyze the components that are involved in the social understanding of what is "real." Here again we can note that certain cultures are predominantly left-hemispheric whereas others are right-hemispheric and that certain societies stress rationalism and empiricism whereas others favor more intuitive modes of knowledge and take for granted what we might call parapsychological phenomena (information-attainment not dependent on the senses). In order for communication to be possible within and between societies there has to be at least a minimal shared body of common knowledge, but we should also keep in mind that each cultural tradition incorporates certain epistemological and linguistic choices that are constitutive of reality perception and selection. It is no exaggeration to say that what is "real" for an American businessman may not be at all so for an American Indian. What a Western scientist holds to be "facts" may be viewed by a Zen Buddhist monk as mere illusion and only superficial, a detour from the "true" pursuit of reality.

It is really not very useful to speak of "reality" yielding facts to an "impartial" observer, because what we see is to a large extent dependent on the manner in which we are predisposed to see, both as societies and as individuals. Indeed, linguists speak of language as not only facilitating but as structuring and directing thought as well:

> Human beings do not live in the objective world alone, nor alone in the world of social activity as ordinarily understood but are very much at the mercy of the particular language which has become the medium of expression for their society. It is quite an illusion to imagine that one adjusts to reality essentially without the use of language and that language is merely an incidental means of solving problems of communication or reflection. The

fact of the matter is that the "real world" is to a large extent unconsciously built up on the language habits of the group, no two languages are ever sufficiently similar to be considered as representing the same social reality. The worlds in which different societies live are distinct worlds, not merely the same world with different labels attached... We see and hear and otherwise experience very largely as we do because the language habits of our community predispose certain choices of interpretation.[11]

The psychologist, the philosopher, the linguist, the sociologist, the scientist, the theologian, and the artist are all concerned with studying the "real" world.[12] Their assumptions and their epistemologies may vary, but it should be kept in mind that no single discipline, no single language pattern or system of knowledge can ever exhaust the human quest to make sense of ourselves and the world around us. It should be clear then, that Freud's definitive statement about the "objective" fact of there being no meaning or value in life is nothing of the sort. He is certainly entitled to his opinion, but it is just that: a personal opinion following from his exclusive reliance on an empirical epistemology. The point to be emphasized is a simple but profound one. If we are not aware of our assumptions about reality and the means we are employing to structure reality, we become like the blind men in the Sufi story. A group of blind men came upon an elephant, an animal they had never encountered before, and began to touch it in various parts. One insisted it was described by its trunk, another by its tail, another by its tusks and yet another by its huge feet. A fifth blind man rejected all these descriptions and said it was obviously understood by its immense ears.

The story is an old one but so too is the wisdom conveyed by it. Any theory of human personality or of the meaning of human existence, which ignores perspectives from other disciplines mirroring other facets of unfathomable reality is incomplete and arrogant.

There is an amusing example of this very point in a recent movie called *The Gods Must Be Crazy*. A bushman tries to return to the "gods" a "gift"—a Coca Cola Bottle tossed out of a plane. His tribe had no word for "bottle" since they had never seen one. During his trek he kills a sheep and is arrested and taken to a courtroom where he is told to enter a plea. In his tribal world there was no such word as "guilty" because everything was owned in common. The tribesman becomes convinced that only lunatics lived in the white person's world.

Medicine tells us that our brain is bifunctional, that it serves different needs at different times and that an integrated personality ideally employs both hemispheres. Biologically and existentially we are incomplete if we are only rational or only intuitive; reality is much richer and vaster than either preference can encompass. One does not have to choose between being realistic *or* religious, between being creative *or* scientific or between whatever categories we employ to partially describe reality.

There should be no conflict, therefore, between religion and science if we understand that they should complement rather than confront each other. That this is not always the case is obvious and we will be better prepared to understand why if we briefly review the shift in ground from a religious framework to a scientific one.

Study Questions

1. In what way would Einstein's idea of God agree and disagree with the God presented in the Jewish Bible?

2. Are you predominantly a right-hemisphere or a left-hemisphere person? How do you decide?

3. Other than in religion, where else do you observe the authoritarian epistemology being employed?

4. Watch a religious service conducted by a TV evangelist. Describe which epistemology is obvious and which is minimized.

5. Do some research on Zen Buddhism. In what ways does their understanding of reality differ from that of our society?

6. Compile a dozen common English words and then look up their equivalent in French. What do you learn about the relationship between language and reality?

Further Readings

1. Fritjof Capra, *The Turning Point* (New York: Bantam Books, 1983).

2. John S. Dunne, *The House of Wisdom* (San Francisco: Harper & Row, 1985).

3. Robert Ornstein, *The Psychology of Consciousness* (San Francisco: W.H. Freeman, 1977).

4. Mary Wolff-Salin, *No Other Light* (New York: Crossroad, 1988).

2.

Religion and Science: The Truth of the Myth

During the process of writing this book I have been interrupted by a woman who came to my door as a representative of a fundamentalist religious group. When I told her I was very familiar with her denomination's teachings and did not accept their biblical fundamentalism* she became very animated and flipped quite rapidly through the Bible to "disprove" my positions. As gently as possible I explained that the scriptures were never meant to be used as a science textbook but rather as a means of understanding God's saving presence in human history. Undaunted, she continued to use the Bible to verify the literal truth of human existence on this planet being limited to 6,000 years, of Noah's ark being large enough to contain all living species of animal during the time of a universal flood, *etc.* I ventured my belief that she was in danger of confusing different levels of meaning and that contemporary Biblical scholars were employing myth and symbol to delve into the fuller message contained within such stories. She was horrified and asked if these scholars believed in God. Evidently the words "myth" and "symbol" were buzz words that she had been warned about in her training program. What do we mean by "symbol" and "myth"?

A "sign" is usually distinguished from a "symbol." A sign is informational and serves to point to something specific or concrete. "Stop," "No Smoking" or "Hospital Zone" convey definite information to the observer. A symbol, while being specific or definite, tends to "point beyond itself" to

9

myth

a wider reality and can convey many different meanings at different times and places. A symbol has the power to link us into a broader understanding of reality. Let us use an example. A "Coke" sign or a "Visa" sign are so common to us that we may be unaware that they are also symbols of a commonly accepted view of reality. The "Coke" sign is universal and communicates many messages: the sophistication of American production methods, the persuasiveness of advertising techniques, the statement that our society has gone far beyond mere survival concerns and can divert resources into relatively superfluous patterns of consumption, *etc*. In many parts of the world such signs as "Coke," "Visa," "Ford," *etc*. are seen as proof of the subtle penetration of American capitalism, materialism, irresponsible consumption of limited natural resources, *etc*. These seemingly harmless signs are viewed by many poor and underdeveloped nations as symbols of affluence and distorted priorities common among citizens of wealthy nations.

It would take us too far afield to fully analyze the American flag as a symbol, but we might ponder the implications of singing the national anthem at sporting events. Does this say something about the way we view life as a people? Is life basically competition, a question of strength and skill, *etc*.? The Olympics have ceased to be merely sports competition and have now assumed political and ideological overtones. The final tabulation of medals is perceived by many persons to say something significant about the relative superiority of differing political systems, much as older Catholics viewed Notre Dame's winning football season as argument for Catholicism's doctrinal positions.

All human disciplines employ symbols which speak of a wider reality in which we participate:

> ... myth, art, language and science appear as symbols; not in the sense of mere figures which refer to some given reality by means of suggestion and allegorical renderings, but in the sense of forces each of which produces and posits a world of its own.... Thus the special symbolic forms are not imitations, but *organs* of reality, since it is solely by their agency that anything real becomes an object for intellectual apprehension, and as such is made visible

to us. The question as to what reality is apart from these forms, and what are its independent attributes, becomes irrelevant here. For the mind, only that can be visible which has some definite form; but every form of existence has its source in some peculiar way of seeing, some intellectual formulation and intuition of meaning. Once language, myth, art and science are recognized as such forms, the basic philosophical question is...that of their mutual limitations and supplementation.[13]

What Cassirer is saying is that science is a symbolic form, but only one of many, which attempts to make sense of reality. The employment of these symbolic forms leads to the development of various, oftentimes competing, "myths" or reality images. Is it accurate to speak of a "scientific myth" or of a "religious myth"?

The common usage of myth refers to something akin to a fairy tale, a pre-scientific or a pre-logical story used by primitives to explain the universe.[14] This popular usage is too limited and ignores those philosophies, ideologies* and systems that have a cosmic dimension. There are "covert" or hidden myths which presume or proclaim the attainment of utopia through technology, the power of human reason to define existence or the inevitability of human progress and happiness. These are really world visions, even if no traditional religious language is used:

When men pool their existentially valid findings and project them out into the universe and ask the ultimate questions of life, when they, in effect, try to encompass the totality of things, they are, in my opinion, offering a mythological statement concerning the nature of reality.[15]

The scientist, the politician, the economist or the psychologist will usually be aware that one is dealing with a relatively limited perspective of reality and that one's specialization deals with proximate or functional questions and not the ultimate ones. The perspective will then be situated within a larger, more encompassing religious, philosophical or humanistic myth that asks the "why" questions rather than just the "how" or "what" questions of daily life. To put it another way, the doctor who can give a highly technical explanation of the medical definition of death must still

wrestle with the meaning of life and the inevitability of one's own death.
Why suffering and death? What happens after death? Medical training
gives no answers to these questions, and so the doctor, like all of us, seeks
a myth that addresses the ultimate questions in accordance with integrity
and intelligence.

The physicist who is comfortable with a world of atomic particles,
curved spaces and energy fields must ponder the question "Why is there
anything?" Like Einstein one might tend to believe that "God does not play
dice with the universe." In any case, we must all seek a tenable myth that
satisfactorily balances a developed curiosity with a sense of awe as we explore the riddles of the material universe.[16] We shall see later that not all
myths offer hope and meaning to human beings but they are myths nonetheless.

Recently, for example, a father was charged with allowing his fourteen
year old son to starve to death. His explanation was that the money he had
belonged to God and that his religious beliefs did not allow him to send his
son to school where he would be fed. This myth of an all-powerful God
who would take care of everything by removing all responsibility for pru-
dent planning had tragic results.

We may confidently say that there need be no conflict between science
and religion unless one or both of these areas intrude upon the other. In
some cases fundamentalists confuse the nature of the Bible and employ it
as a science book. There is an overly concrete and extremely literal understanding of biblical texts, outside the context of any historical, theological,
or linguistic frame of reference, which becomes the rule of faith. Symbols,
which should point to an ineffable* reality which is never fully contained
by word or thought, are frozen in what the great student of religion Mircea
Eliade, calls "a process of infantilization." This can come about by the
symbol becoming a substitute for the sacred object or a means of establishing a relationship with it.[17] As the Protestant theologian, Paul Tillich,
put it, a religious symbol is idolatrous unless it suggests its own inadequacy.[18]

How can this happen? If we take Adam and Eve to have been actual
historical persons, Noah's Ark to have been an actual floating zoo or the

altend → obstacle

six days of creation mentioned in Genesis to be literal calendar days, the literal interpretation becomes an obstacle to understanding the deeper message of faith contained in the symbol. This is precisely what Eliade and Tillich are criticizing.

I hope it is clear that we understand that certain religious traditions have, at different times in history, confused the message of salvation with the medium of human symbols and felt the need to attack scientific advances. This antagonism, unfortunately, was also manifested by certain individuals who purported to use science as a means of creating a "superior" rationalistic myth. These persons confused the medium of limited conceptual constructs for the message of a comprehensive world view. This is a process often called "scientism,"* the tendency to take limited knowledge of the natural world and expand it into a statement about ultimate reality. Akin to this is "reductionism,"* the simplistic treatment of a complex phenomenon in a very limited way. The psychologist Sigmund Freud reduced religion to a kind of childhood neurosis[19] whereas the sociologist, Emile Durkheim reduced religion to nothing more than society's common value system.[20] They confused function with origin, believing that if they could analyze its role in individual and social life they were explaining how religion originated. Since neither man believed in God their treatment of religion could not allow for the possibility that religion arises because God exists. Benighted believers and dogmatic natural and social scientists did little to create an atmosphere for intelligent and beneficial dialogue.

The role of a scientific myth or paradigm is to generate theories that introduce meaning into the raw data of observation. The role of a religious myth is to foster beliefs which help to make sense of common human experiences. Religion should not find itself in conflict with science. Religion needs science to aid it in avoiding misinterpreting natural phenomena in a supernatural or magical fashion. As the Jesuit paleontologist,* Pierre Teillhard de Chardin often noted, the development within all fields of human knowledge is part of God's plan for our God-given intelligence. There should be no fear of unfolding knowledge on religion's part, although historically such advances have forced a re-evaluation and reinterpretation of certain religious teachings. Such purification is both healthy and necessary.

It may be healthy and necessary, but it is not always easy. I remember one very conservative seminary teacher who was adamantly opposed to evolution, telling the class, "If you want to believe your great grandfather was a clam, that's your business." He judged that evolution denied human dignity and, in the process, made for a very strange family tree.

Science has gradually and oftentimes begrudgingly come to recognize the need for external criteria in many sensitive and potentially dangerous areas of investigation. Robert Oppenheimer, one of the major American physicists involved in developing atomic energy lamented, when the atomic bomb was dropped, that "science has known original sin." In the same sober vein, the Nobel prize winner, Albert von Szent-Gyorgi, looked back on his life as a scientist and observed that all scientists run the risk of seeing their every discovery and breakthrough co-opted by the military establishment in every nation.[21]

One need not agree with the latter's harsh indictment, but it is becoming clear that "value free" scientific investigation is a fiction, one belatedly admitted by the social sciences as well. The larger framework to which religion attends, that of ends and not just means, is increasingly more crucial as we develop the techniques for altering or even destroying life on this planet. We come full circle to the Genesis myth of Adam and Eve, finding that we, as a society, have eaten of the tree of knowledge and must now discern the difference between good and evil. Religion serves to remind us of our human fallibility, of our need to correlate our science with a vision of persons that is grounded in a Reality beyond any human reckoning. We need to know the difference between knowledge and wisdom:

> The giant computers and gleaming laboratories are of no use whatever in telling us the proper ends of human endeavor. Science and faith do not now contend for the same domain, and faith is undiminished by the growth of science. Science has disencumbered man's religious disposition of mistaken myths about the material universe without lessening the degree to which life proceeds on something dark and deep and, however clothed in the garb of reason, arbitrary. All our ends are lodged in faith, science

helps us with means. All the great and fundamental questions are answered, if at all, only by faith. What is important in life? What is worth struggling for, and how much? Should I love my neighbor, concern myself with his suffering?. . .Shall I accept violence and murder as necessary to man's life and arm myself accordingly, or shall I declare them elective and work for their elimination? Shall I listen to those who say I can do both? The computers are silent, the test tubes do not react to these queries. . .[22]

Both religion and science are concerned with explanations of reality; both are attempts to make sense of the world in which we live. Science deals with the material world and emphasizes the epistemologies of empiricism and rationalism. It is concerned with detecting orderly and coherent patterns within a mass of observable data. The scientist has a specific and limited focus and does not presume to speak of the "nature of reality" but rather of one important dimension of it. In response to the existence of determinism* (cause and effect correlations) in classical physics, the philosopher of science, Karl R. Popper noted:

I suggest that this misinterpretation is due to the tendency of attributing to Science (with a capital S) a kind of omniscience; and that this theological view of science ought to be replaced by a more humanistic view, by the realization that science is the work of ordinary humans groping their way in the dark. In doing so, we may sometimes find something interesting; we may be astonishingly successful; but we should never get anything like "the whole truth." Our theories are not descriptions of nature, but only of some little feathers which we have plucked out of nature's garb more or less accidentally.[23]

There are questions that science, regardless of the personal positions of individual scientists, cannot presume to answer because they lie beyond its limited and specific competence. Likewise, religion is not qualified to pass judgment on the veracity of scientific theories but must limit itself to the qualitative questions having to do with practical applications of such theories. In such ways religion and science complement each other and provide a necessary corrective to the temptations of unreflective piosity* on the one hand and of arrogant dogmatism* on the other. Religion and science are human systems that attempt to explore the world and make sense of our human experiences, neither one of which is complete without the other. All human questing, religious, scientific or whatever, is basically an attempt to understand ourselves and to know what is "real." The day should be long past when any one approach to reality is considered to be the exclusive pathway. The traditional squabbles between religion and science should now give way to patterns of cooperation and humble recognition of their respective limitations and specific competencies.[24]

Glossary

Determinism is a philosophy that rejects free will and holds that all effects are the result of causes beyond human control.

Dogmatism is the assertion that one's position is absolute truth.

Fundamentalism is a religious position that rigidly adheres to certain basic principles and rejects modern liberal thought that would claim to modify or update belief. It holds to a literal interpretation of scripture.

Ideology refers to ideas supporting the vested interests of an individual or group. It is a form of dogmatism.

Ineffable means something cannot be easily or adequately expressed or described.

Paleontologists study bones, leaf imprints, *etc.* in order to understand the past.

Piosity is the exaggerated expression of religious feeling or devotion.

Reductionism is the attempt to explain complex phenomena by a single explanation. For example, love is reduced to hormonal reactions.

Scientism is a form of reductionism whereby everything is explained by the methods used in the physical sciences.

Study Questions

1. Why do Americans burn or bury their old flags whereas other nationalities simply throw them away?

2. In what important ways do science and religion need each other to avoid reaching partial answers?

3. Why are so many religious fundamentalists suspicious of science?

4. Which myths do you think are most popular in the United States today ? Which ones shape your own reality?

5. Do some research on the Scopes "monkey trial" of 1925. What were the issues involved and where do you see the same issues being debated today?

6. Research the condemnation of Galileo. Why did it happen?

Further Reading

1. Ian G. Barbour, *Myths, Models, and Paradigms* (New York: Harper and Row, 1976).

2. Don Cupitt, *The Worlds of Science and Religion* (New York: Hawthorne Books, 1976).

3. Arthur Koestler, *Janus* (New York: Vintage Books, 1979).

4. Donald M. MacKay, *Science and the Quest for Meaning* (Grand Rapids: Eerdmans, 1982).

5. Alfred North Whitehead, *Science and the Modern World* (New York: Free Press, 1925).

3.

Atheism and Agnosticism: Alternative Myths

The character of an age and the most dominant—even if only implicit—social attitudes of a society are reflected in the vision individuals have of themselves and their relation to the world. Socialization and individuation are really complementary processes. Prior to the Copernican revolution people visualized their planet as the center of the universe and maintained their cosmology with some sort of theological system. Reason was the handmaid of revelation.

Copernicus, Galileo, Newton, Darwin, Freud, Marx, *etc.* have helped shape a vastly different cosmology, and each, ironically, has contributed to a schizophrenic* self-image for contemporary Westerners. No longer viewed as the center of the universe or the object of theistic* pampering, we are reduced in stature, while, at the same time, our rational functions are the putative means for unlocking all the mysteries of the universe and we are presumed infinite through our activities. Reason replaced the gods.

Nature came to be regarded as a mechanism, a part of a coherent cosmic order governed by law, and we, as a part of nature, came to be defined in terms of the very same laws which controlled our development and that of society. Gradually we became an object of our own study, an entity among entities, expressed in, and limited by, impersonal laws. There has been a long history of dualism, the body/soul or matter/spirit problem, in both Eastern and Western thought. In the West, the stage was set for the reloca-tion of the soul from the pineal gland (Descartes) to the unconscious depths (Freud) or to the chemicals of the brain (Skinner); Spirit became matter in the process and it became fashionable to reduce the human person, along with the environment, to a collection of drives, atoms, reflexes and dialectics, the better to study humans objectively.[25] There has been a concomitant tendency to devaluate the "merely" personal or subjective perspective, because it was not "scientific" or objectively verifiable:

> Still there is nothing in the world of experience labeled "data" or "reality." We must select those things we want to notice. Our own culture, by and large, selects those things that are countable, analyzable, and most easily accessible to prediction and control. We are, as every culture is, entitled to call "real" what we so select. But we are obliged, as other cultures, to note that our "reality" is but one selection from the rich texture of human experience—even of our own experience. In our most advanced sciences, like physics, these points are well known. What the scientist knows is not "reality," pure and simple, but the answers he gets back to the questions he elects to raise. He gets back to a disturbing extent, a reflection of his own interests, procedures, and imagined models...
>
> Since our personal sense of reality is tutored by the culture in which we live, we are obliged to notice the ways in which education directs our attention to those "facts" suitable for scientific procedures. Experiences of ours—mystical, personal, intuitive, instinctive, groping—which are not "hard" or "objective," our teachers insinuate, are beneath our notice, unreliable, dangerous: "Oh, but you're making a value judgment!" is sometimes considered a put-down.[26]

Novak clearly states the need to reflect on the very basic fact that our view of reality, our definition of "normal," our selection of the optimal state of consciousness for most efficient functioning is neither true nor false, but rather functional or dysfunctional within a given society. What we consider real, reflects to a large extent, what we consider important. If we value only rational and empirical epistemologies then art, music, religion, literature, feeling, *etc.* will be judged as superfluous when dealing with the "real" world. Some futurologists* take for granted that we will live in a "surprise-free" world and that "practical" concerns will be universally pursued.[27]

An issue of *Life* magazine in the 1950s predicted the "City of the Future." It showed gleaming high-rise buildings connected by climate controlled ramps and orderly traffic patterns as electric cars flowed quietly and cleanly past pedestrians on moving sidewalks. The actual condition of American cities as we approach the end of the 20th century shows that futurology is a risky business.

Such predictions are not new but merely unimaginative in that they presume a very limited ability to alter present patterns of activity. There is a religious saying that holds that "since there is a God, tomorrow can be different." We might also suggest that since human beings are not computers or robots, certain trends notwithstanding, a "surprise-free" world is based on a conception of the human person roughly equivalent to that of an intellectual lemming.

Mechanism (humans as machines), materialism (humans as matter), and determinism (humans as products of the environment) are the more common ideologies and theories erected to reduce the complex and rather unpredictable human personality to a tidy and observable package. This kind of pseudo-science has a long history and ultimately reflects a belief in our newest myth, that of human self-sufficiency apart from any recognition of, or need for, an Other. One explicit form of this myth is atheism, a certainty that there is no God.

In Psalm 14 of the Bible we read: "The fool says in his heart: 'There is no God.'" It is likely that atheism has existed side by side with belief in a God or gods from the very beginning of human consciousness. What is peculiar to our age, at least since the Renaissance* period, is a definite lessening of social support for religious viewpoints. We are told by historians and sociologists that we live in a "secularized" world. Secularization* has generally been taken to mean a shift in human perspective and concern from the "other-worldly" to the "this-worldly," a decline in the influence of organized religion (in fact, if not always in appearance) and the ascendency of science, reason and scepticism over revelation, metaphysics* and religious authoritarianism. It would take another book to make the needed qualifications and distinctions within such a generalization, but it seems true to state that the religious attitude is considerably more difficult to sustain for persons in our era than in previous ones.[28] Let us examine some of the arguments atheism has presented.

1. *Rationalism*—Reason alone is the criterion for truth. Since religion is based on faith and cannot be proven, it goes beyond reason and is ultimately an insult to human intelligence. Some rationalists, however, were willing to accept religion as long as it was cleansed of all supernatural elements. A personal God, revelation, inspired scriptures, miracles, *etc.* had to be rejected if they could not be verified by human reason. The philosopher David Hume (1711-76) exemplified this position by treating miracles as impossible violations of the laws of nature.[29]

2. *Existentialism*—It is a bit difficult to neatly characterize this viewpoint since it has different meanings for the atheist and for the Christian who embrace it, but the works of the writer Franz Kafka (1883-1924) and the philosopher Jean-Paul Sartre (1905-80) are representative of its original focus. In *The Trial* by Kafka and in *No Exit* by Sartre we enter the existentialist world of alienation,* absurdity and despair. Each person must create his own meaning and resist the temptation to rely on others for making choices: God, the "Unstared Stare," who sees us but is not seen by us in return, is an enemy of freedom. If there existed an absolute and universal order of values, we would be coerced to judge ourselves by someone else's (God's) decision. For Sartre, "bad faith" is the surrendering of our responsibility to others, and God is the ultimate annihilator of freedom, a foe to be resisted at all costs:

> ...martyrdom, salvation, and immortality are falling to pieces; the edifice is going to rack and ruin; I collared the Holy Ghost in the cellar and threw him out; atheism is a cruel and long-range affair; I think I've carried it through; I see clearly, I've lost my illusions, I know what my real jobs are, I surely deserve a prize for good citizenship.[30]

3. *Value*—Some individuals view God and religion as supportive of mediocrity, dependence, and of the "weak" virtues of simplicity, humility, patience, compassion and resignation. Perhaps one of the major spokespersons for this position was Frederick Nietzsche (1844-1900), the tormented philosopher, who spoke of the "death of God" and the emergence of the "superman" whose autonomy would be based on the "will to power." Nietzsche especially despised Christianity and its stress on God's providence: "Religion has debased the notion of man; its extreme consequence is that all good, all greatness, all truth are superhuman and given to man by grace."[31] Simply put, God's existence is seen as a threat to human autonomy and dignity and as a galling reminder of the limits of human existence, of our dependent "creaturehood."[32]

4. *Marxism*—Karl Marx (1818-83) was a Jew, a descendant of generations of rabbis, whose father converted to Lutheranism for reasons of sheer expediency, as his son judged, baptizing Karl at age six in order to enable him to enter public school. Marx's family was only nominally Christian during his rearing. More important than this personal disdain, however, Marx became convinced that religion, especially Protestantism which he linked to capitalism, was an obstacle to human progress. An optimist, Marx was a firm believer in a paradise on earth and he was just as firmly certain that religion supported unjust economic systems and countenanced passive acceptance of the *status quo* while promising a future reward in the afterlife. He scoffed at this as "pie-in-the-sky" thinking. Religion, for Marx, was the "opiate of the people," an instrument used by the dominant capitalist* class to maintain its power to exploit the workers. There was no need to persecute religion because once the true economic nature of all reality was understood, religion would simply disappear. Marx believed that the existence of religion was the proof of a society's social injustice.[33]

It is interesting to note that in 1988 Mikhail Gorbachev, general secretary of the Soviet communist party, returned monasteries and churches to the Russian Orthodox Church on the occasion of its celebration of 1,000 years of Christianity in the Soviet Union. The Church is attracting the young in growing numbers, an indication perhaps that Marx was not a very accurate futurologist.

5. *Suffering*—No doubt many of the preceding reasons and arguments given for atheism may strike the average student as the limited concerns of theoreticians, or as reflections of historical circumstances that no longer hold. There is, however, a common experience that moves us beyond mere intellectual debating into the heart of the matter of religion and/or God: the inevitability of pain, disappointment, sorrow, depression, etc., not just in the abstract but in our own lives and in those of others. The sight of a child suffering from leukemia; the senseless acts of violence that plague the elderly and defenseless throughout our country; the interminable slaughters carried out in the name of nationalism,* religion, politics, economics or whatever, in various parts of the world, cause grave difficulty for many persons who seek to integrate belief in a loving God or an Ultimate Reality* with the chaos and destruction that is everywhere apparent. Most religions have developed theodicies, or systems of theological reflection that attempt to mesh belief in divine justice with the existence of suffering. We shall look at these answers later but presently it is sufficient to note that the problem of suffering is central to all myths and is one that admits of no simple resolution.[34]

6. *The Irreligion of the Religious*—Although the truth or falsity of any position should not logically depend on those who claim to represent it, but rather on the dispassionate analysis of the premises themselves, we are all susceptible to our own first impressions. Representatives of various minority groups are extremely sensitive on this point for they fully appreciate the ease with which an obnoxious, flamboyant or arrogant spokesperson can deflect attention from the cause to the commotion. In much the same way, religion and God are often at the mercy of those who claim to be religious. Many individuals cannot seriously consider the God question when confronted with believers who appear smug, self-righteous, narrow-minded or intolerant. Worse still is the so-called believer whose life, actions and speech betray no appreciable reflection of claimed religious convictions. In other words, if belief in God or religious practice seems to make one no different from the person who does not believe or practice, they wonder, "Why all the fuss?"[35]

I remember studying in Canada at the time of Vice President Spiro Agnew's disgraced exit from office and the tedious unwinding of the web of deceit and criminal activity entangling President Nixon and his *coterie* of supporters. A friend asked how I could be proud of the United States when corruption was so pervasive. I replied that the ideals and vision of the Republic may have been tarnished and distorted by these men but that it was unthinkable that my country was accurately imaged by these self-serving individuals. I was saddened but still convinced of the American promise. The same is true for religion and God no matter how poorly served by their partisans.* This is not to eschew justifiable criticism but rather to nudge the discussion back to its central focus. We shall later return to this point in some concluding observations.

A final group of individuals who cannot accept a religious myth are called agnostics. An agnostic is one who is undecided about God's existence; one who is not able to accept or reject God, having less certitude than either the believer or the atheist. Agnosticism strikes me as an uneasy and transient stand, one difficult to maintain indefinitely. It may be either an indication of fuzzy thinking (some persons seem to always choose "undecided" when polled on issues) or a sign of honest and painful searching for answers.

One of the more recent treatments of agnosticism is found in Peter Schaffer's play *Equus*. The story can be read on many levels, and, while not terribly profound, it is a moving statement about the anguish of many contemporary thinkers. The psychiatrist, Dr. Dysart, is called upon to "cure" a young man responsible for blinding a number of horses. As the action progresses, it becomes clear to Dr. Dysart that he does not really have a vital and comprehensive personal myth. Religion, as symbolized by the boy's mother, and atheism, as stereotyped by the boy's father, are sterile and unattractive positions. So too, however, is the new "religion of sanity," the myth of sweet reason. The distraught psychiatrist comes to envy the boy's passion and vitality, regardless of its eventual culmination in mutilation, because the boy believed in something. If it is no longer possible for Dr. Dysart to have the consolation, simplicity and sureness of absolute faith, he also cannot live the prevalent myth of well-adjusted, reasonable, sane, lifeless normalcy. Many psychiatrists would concur that Dr. Dysart is commonly encountered in their own clients who are seeking to make some overall sense of the bits and pieces that life appears to be.[36]

Reflections

How one chooses to live in this world and what one comes to value, to notice, to celebrate, to treasure—in short, what kind of myth one puts faith in—is the result of a congeries of factors. Our parents, our education, our friends, even our enemies, significant others, whether known first-hand or not, our sensitivity to the world around us, our ability to be quiet with ourselves—all of these elements and more are ingredients in our unique biography. Joy and sorrow, suffering and pleasure, accomplishment and disappointment are interwoven into the lives of each person, whether one believes in a God or not. To think that any system, religious, scientific or humanistic, can be absorbed by osmosis* and thus spare us the effort to be reflective and critical about our own meaning as human beings and the purpose of life itself is most naive.

When I taught high school the chaplains required each class to attend a weekly Mass in the auditorium. They felt these young men would somehow become "more Catholic" when the liturgy was being conducted. Many students, by their own admission, simply counted this as Sunday obligation and did not attend their parish church. I learned from this that there is no "magical" shortcut to personal faith apart from one's lived experience.

All religions insist that life is a gift from a source beyond ourselves, that existence is not mere accident and happenstance, that it is purposeful. Our science, art, music, philosophy, literature, social sciences and our religions are so many approaches, consciously employed or not, of asking questions basic to all human beings. What does life mean? What is most important? How, if at all, does it come together? Different epistemologies, different languages and different disciplines all contribute to the mosaic. All religions insist that there is more, a wider, deeper, mysterious backdrop against which all of our partial approaches, including religion, must be understood.

The religious myth serves a number of functions:[37]

1. It helps make sense of the experience of wonder, awe, mystery, of limitation and of our own mortality. While not everyone is open to all of these experiences to the same extent, it is unlikely that anyone is totally immune from such feelings at sometime in life.

2. It provides a moral dimension to life by calling forth adult responsibility for our own lives and reflection upon the dignity of others who share the gift of life. Religion is not just a question of belief but of behavior consonant with that belief.

3. It helps make sense of guilt and failure, both universal experiences. All of us at some time or another act against our own values or make choices that harm ourselves or others. Religion can offer hope for our anxiety and self-deprecation and give us the courage to accept ourselves.[38]

4. It can provide an identity that is more than personal or egocentric. Religion calls us out of our narrow, self-centered existence into a transcendent relationship with the Other and others. Religion also provides a needed dimension of humility by reminding us that all human projects require constant evaluation within the context of values that are not gratuitously bestowed by human beings on one another. Religion, in brief, calls us to community with others and speaks of a shared humanity.[39]

Religion provides meaning and it also provides security. If, however, the security is maintained at the expense of our desire to know or of our insight into ourselves, it becomes a crutch and is unworthy of a mature individual. To reiterate: our religion, if it is vital and authentic, is able to integrate new insights and knowledge from various sources and to expand our understanding of reality. If we believe, as Jesus said, that the truth will make us free, there need be no fear for healthy religion encountering new ideas. St. Thomas Aquinas noted that truth, from whatever source, comes from the Holy Spirit, so self-deception need never be the price paid to achieve security. What we believe need not challenge what we know but should lead us to reflect upon the deeper meanings within our religious myth.

Religious persons are sometimes tempted to become very defensive, even belligerent, when an atheist or an agnostic questions their positions. Hate letters flood the newspapers whenever Madeline Murray O'Hare* files suit to remove public recognition of religion in various institutions. Such extreme reaction suggests deep-seated insecurity and fear and more than a passing suspicion that such venom reflects belief in a God akin to a bloodthirsty Aztec deity.

The atheist and the agnostic can aid the believer to question what it is one truly believes, to analyze one's own religious myth to see if it incorporates superstition, magic or even ignorance. These dissenters can be purifying catalysts if they point out inconsistencies in behavior and professed belief. The believer who is intolerant of other viewpoints or positions may be helped by a challenger to see that belief in God should never lead to hatred or derision unless the religious myth is inadequate. If, as the atheist suggests, religion is unworthy of an intelligent person, believers may be aided in rethinking and reaffirming their deepest commitments. Only pseudo-religion or mere convention need fear such questions.

In like fashion, the agnostic may legitimately inquire if religion is not used as an escape from reality and from the complex struggle for making sense of life. If the believer appears to be smugly self-confident of all the answers when life appears to admit of no such easy certitude, the agnostic may serve to reintroduce the awareness of the Hidden God who is present in our midst but never contained within any neat formula or any book or ritual. Anything human, religion included, is in need of reform and is an imperfect vehicle for human self-understanding. If God or the absolute is the end of all religious myths, atheists and agnostics can serve to caution us against an idolatrous employment of the means to reach that goal:

> The general point remains that man is a mystery to himself. In the darkness of that mystery, he does not know for certain whether to be cautious or to adore. Either way, he falls short of seeing God. We cannot directly make ourselves experience God.

If we "experience" him at all, it is by a sort of indirection, by a quietness and unity and complacence (overlooking creation and seeing: "It is good") that steals over us by a dark communion.[40]

The myth within which we live is a risk, a choice among choices, a reflection of what we imagine life to be about. A myth expresses our self-understanding as well and is based on the most comprehensive and least easily surrendered choices life has to offer, but for a myth to be realistic and meaningful it must be true to our own deepest experiences.

Glossary

Alienation is literally the condition of being a stranger to oneself and others.

Capitalists are those who favor competition in a free market system and the private ownership and control of wealth. The profit motive drives this economic system.

Futurologists are social scientists who attempt to predict future patterns based upon a careful study of present economic, historical and political trends.

Madeline Murray O'Hare is a prominent and outspoken atheist who advocates restricting the public role and privilege of religion.

Metaphysics is a branch of philosophy concerned with theoretical and speculative questions like being, truth, reality, *etc*.

Nationalism focuses on the interests of a particular culture or nation over international goals.

Osmosis is a gradual, often unconscious, assimilation or absorption of something, *e.g.*, language.

Partisans are devoted followers of a cause or person.

Renaissance means "rebirth" and refers to a revival of interest in ancient Greek and Roman culture among western Europeans from the 14th to 16th centuries.

Schizophrenia is an ambiguous medical term that is commonly used to describe a split personality or a withdrawal from reality.

Secularization is the process of removing religion from public life and restricting it to a matter of private concern.

Theistic means belief in a personal God.

Ultimate Reality is that which is final and complete. Nothing greater can be comprehended.

Study Questions

1. Which argument for atheism do you think is most convincing? What response can religion make?

2. Reflect upon your own religious beliefs. How well do the four functions of religious myth apply?

3. Do you think an atheist could ever be elected President of the United States? Why or why not?

4. Read *Equus* by Peter Schaffer. Discuss the religious roots of the young man's problem.

5. What is the appeal of Marxism? Why has it been so hostile to religion of any kind?

6. Study the life of Charles Darwin. Why did many religious leaders attack his findings?

Further Readings

1. Bernard Basset, *We Agnostics* (New York: Herder & Herder, 1968).

2. Robert MacAfee Brown, *Is Faith Obsolete?* (Philadelphia: Westminster Press, 1974).

3. Howard R. Burkle, *God, Suffering, and Belief* (Nashville: Abingdon, 1977).

4. Richard E. Creel, *Religion and Doubt: Toward a Faith of Your Own* (Englewood Cliffs, NJ: Prentice-Hall, 1977).

5. Ignace Lepp, *Atheism in our Time,* trans. Bernard Murchland (New York: Macmillan, 1963).

4.

Experience:
The Basis of Myth

In some philosophical and scientific quarters the word *experience* has been denigrated as some kind of "mental" construct or a merely personal feeling located within, and limited to, individual consciousness. It has often been viewed as unscientific, vague, parochial or untrustworthy. Such judgments bespeak a basic misunderstanding of what experience is.

The psychologist Carl Rogers insists, for example, that the *only* thing of which we can be certain is our own experience:

> Experience is, for me, the highest authority. The touchstone of validity is my own experience. No other person's ideas and none of my own ideas, are as authoritative as my experience. It is to experience that I must return again and again to discover a closer approximation to truth as it is in the process of becoming in me.[41]

What Rogers and others mean by experience is far more profound than just an idea or an "encounter" with someone or something. Experience should be viewed as the relationship between persons who ask questions of themselves and of the world around them, and of an objective reality which does not depend upon them for its existence. An encounter, on the other hand, is merely the first step in the experiencing process. An encounter deals with the surface of an object, experience with the depth.[42] Experience requires various interactions between ourselves and that which is encountered. This helps explain why two individuals may have diametrically opposed evaluations of the same person. It is the difference between

31

an acquaintance and a friend. An acquaintance sees our surface self, but a true friend knows us in depth.

When we speak of experience, then, we are really speaking of the only way we have of knowing reality at all. Michael Polanyi, in attempting to produce a radically original view of knowledge in science, has concisely addressed himself to this position:

> For, as human beings, we must inevitably see the universe from a center lying within ourselves and speak about it in terms of a human language shaped by the exigencies of human intercourse. Any attempt rigorously to eliminate our human perspective from our picture of the world must lead to absurdity.[43]

Polanyi makes a crucial distinction between the *personal,* which is a commitment of one's being to something believed in, and the *subjective,* which is simply in the nature of a condition of being. If a person does not personally believe in something, has not integrated it into one's own experience, is not committed to it, what eventuates is not knowledge but facts or allegations of knowledge.[44] In terms of religion, the experience must be a personal one if it is to be more than a philosophy of religion or detached speculation about God or the meaning of existence:

> The reality of God from the religious standpoint means the answering of the question about the ground and purpose of human life. Failure to understand this point is a major factor in the perpetuation of merely conventional religion in which belief in God is either the fulfillment of a duty imposed by an institution or the inert belief that, in addition to all the finite things that exist, there is one more existent being called "God."[45]

If the religious object[46] is not personally experienced but merely assented to, then religion becomes no more vital than belief in plane geometry or life on other planets. Interesting or possible, perhaps, but of no immediate or practical value. We shall see how this applies to the distinction between mature and immature religion.

no exclusiveness

TRUTH

Experience is both objective and subjective. Subjective, because it is a reality involving a knower, and objective, because it involves something known. Experience, thus understood, is the only way we have of knowing anything at all, of relating to external reality. Even as it is presupposed that individual perceptions must be correlated, to some degree, with those of others, care must be taken to respect the uniqueness of individual experience. Once we move beyond scientific knowledge which is, for the most part, empirically verifiable, into the more fluid areas of the humanities, art, and religion, general consensus on the facts of experience is less easily obtained. Experience, religious and otherwise, involves frameworks of meaning within which what we encounter is interpreted and evaluated. The tools for interpreting will be our various disciplines—psychology, theology, sociology, history, science, logic, *etc.*, employing various epistemologies. No one is exclusive but rather they are so many viewpoints for understanding the things of the world.

There are two historical theories about how we know anything. At one pole is *gnosticism*, a philosophy which taught that the object of our experience is immediately intuited without recourse to logical analysis or reflection. The classical philosophical mystic, Plotinus, spoke of the "flight of the alone to the alone," and the final insight as the apprehension of the One "with nothing in between." We shall see that such a path is the one favored by various forms of Buddhism and by mystics in every religious tradition. Sometimes intellectually lazy or flaky types find this an attractive approach to knowledge. They pick up "vibes" or "groove" into a viewpoint. Gnosticism has historically embraced both the great mystics and the "Oh, Wow!" types.

At the other pole is *empiricism*, which holds that the object of experience must be attainable through the senses to be known. At most, we can only infer, but not directly experience, what we cannot touch, taste, hear, see or smell. This position is comically exemplified by the Russian cosmonaut who returned to earth and proclaimed to the press that he had disproved God's existence because, on looking out of his spaceship, he had not seen anyone in outer space.

The point is that personal experience is a trustworthy and reliable pathway to reality, requiring, at the same time, the arduous task of seeking for patterns of intelligibility and understanding within the experience. In the case of the religious dimension of experience, the believer is challenged to evaluate and interpret that experience. There is the risk of faith in trusting our experience in religious convictions, but the risk is not an irrational one, anymore than the one involved in a love relationship.

When two persons are in love they are aware that the bond they share can, to some extent, be logically analyzed and verbalized, but because they are involved at deeper levels than the intellectual, there is a mutual commitment of their personhood in many subtle and often ineffable dimensions. To attempt to sit down and draw up a list of "reasons" why two persons are in love will be futile in trying to fully encompass the richness of the bond. This is why some persons seem incapable of entering into a rich relationship with others: they are so detached at observing others that they never risk their total being with another at levels and in ways that are often groping, mysterious, and ambiguous. So, too, in religious experience there are persons who demand logical proofs for God's existence rather than risking entering into the personal experience of mystery, awe, dependence and wonder.

The intelligent person must reflect upon one's relationship with the other, analyzing the meaning and intensity of the shared existence, if only to detect elements of fantasy, wish-fulfillment or self-deception. The same is true in our relationship to our religious object, but we can no more "think" ourselves into love than we can "prove" our way into a religious experience. In any case, we must be true to our own personal experience, as thinking, feeling, reflective, complex individuals who are involved at many levels of ourselves with another or the Other.

We may eventually find we were mistaken in our love or simply untrue to ourselves in our religious quest. To refuse or risk love or a religious experience because we may be wrong is to refuse to meet life on its own terms. When two persons have a deep and trusting relationship they discover dimensions and insights about each other that may have been hidden when they were separate personalities. True love has the very real power to call the other into being, to give the courage to accept and respect ourselves because we see ourselves through someone else's life. That so many couples remain virtual strangers to each other even after many years of marriage, testifies to the fear of self-disclosure[47] many persons exhibit. They may well be unaware of the other person's deepest feelings, needs, fears and desires because they observe but do not really participate in the life of the other person, except in a routine and self-centered way.

Within the religious dimension of experience the same atrophy* may ensue, for a variety of reasons. Our experience may be second-hand or a merely routine expression of what we have been taught but which has not ever caught fire within our own lives. Our religious experience may be more notional than personal, much like the person who says, "yeah, I'm married" in a tone indicating a fact more than a conviction. Going back to Polanyi's distinction, the experience is subjective but not really personal.

In love, as in religion, we can learn to distrust our own experience and defer to the "experts." Some individuals do not marry the person of their choice because Mommy, Daddy or their friends give "facts" to dissuade him or her. I have dear friends who underwent such a trauma when they approached their families with the person they loved. He is a white man from a very tightly-knit ethnic neighborhood and she is a black woman from an equally close kinship background. All of the very considerable arguments were mustered by both families to make them relent: American society is highly color-conscious; their children will have problems in school; housing opportunities will be limited; in moments of anger their own culturally conditioned biases will flare into the open and cause festering wounds, *etc.* They knew all these things, of course, and tried to explain that their love was strong enough to withstand these pressures, or at least, they were willing to risk everything because they experienced a love that could not be understood only on "reasonable" grounds by a third party. The end result was that they married, were disowned by their families and now inhabit a world where they seek to experience persons instead of racial categories. They are happy because they trusted their experience of love rather than their family's experience of prejudice. There is no suggestion here of flying in the face of social reality but rather of indicating that experience is far more than a matter of detached logic. Their decision did not ignore their parents' facts but rather incorporated and went beyond them as the basis for their commitment.

Another example: a friend of mine teaches at a prestigious Ivy League university. He recounts with great amusement the inevitable reaction from his colleagues when they learn he is a practicing Catholic and attends church regularly. They are disconcerted because the common wisdom holds that religion is the private preserve of the uneducated and superstitious, and no reputable academics should be skulking around monuments from the pre-Enlightenment* era. My friend judges that they are common victims of a positivistic[48] education and are approaching religion from what they have read and not from personal experience. He believes that their theories have shriveled their experiential possibilities and trapped them in very limited paradigms.[49]

What becomes most clear in the treatment of experience—and perhaps most especially for its religious dimension—is that another person can only surmise that it approximates one's own experience and lends itself to one's own categories of interpretation.[50] The real danger is that explanation becomes distortion.

The predilection to group persons into convenient slots and then to assign motivations or to attempt to definitively analyze something as personal and complex as the religious experience is a constant temptation. There is precious little neutral ground available upon which to stand when one talks of one's own religious experience or that of another; too much of who we are, or perceive ourselves to be, is interwoven into such an undertaking. It is a wise observation that applies to all, psychologists or not, who try to cloak themselves in a mantle of impartiality:

> A psychologist's interpretation of the religious experience and the place of religious belief in personality change depends more often than he realizes, on methodological presuppositions, and his conception of truth, of value, and of reality.[51]

The psychologist, sociologist, philosopher of religion and the theologian may well judge that the observed behavior of a person claiming belief in God or a transcendent dimension to life manifests varying degrees of escapism, infantile dependency, personality integration, maturity, or whatever phrases express his own school of thought. We commit a common, but nonetheless egregious error if we think we are therefore justified in speaking of the "proof" or lack of it for God or whatever description of ultimate reality the person claims to experience or reject. In the final analysis, an examination of the experiencing process can give no definitive judgment of the object of religious experience.[52] It is for this reason that I avoid the quagmire of so-called "proofs" for theism or atheism or the validity and authenticity of religion, focusing instead on the understanding of the religious dimension of experience as shared by major religious figures. In the final analysis, each person must reflect on whether it speaks to one's own experience or not. No one else can "give" us a religious experience but can only invite us to see things from a particular perspective and to be open to our own depths.

Both believer and sceptic are free to deny that such is their personal experience or even of their understanding of religious experience; they are on the brink of audacity when they insist that one who claims that such an understanding of one's religious experience is personally authentic and viable is actually deluded or inaccurate. The very nature of religious experience should lead us to reflect:

> What difference is there, then, between a man who refuses to name God or to "believe" in him even though he is scrupulously faithful to understanding, cherishes friendships, values creativity—and a man who through the same fidelity, experience of friendship and hunger to create does give a name to God and does believe that he exists? Both men live a life similar in nearly every respect. Secular saint and religious saint alike strive to diminish the amount of suffering in the world; neither one sees God. One says Yes to understanding, love, creativity, but No to God. The other thinks that the first yes implies the second.[53]

The divergence in understanding religious experience or one's own humanity should not lull us into overlooking the fact that many persons will live and die for their convictions and that their integrity and self-respect will not allow them to pretend that it is inconsequential how one answers Novak's question. These committed individuals may further seek to "enlighten" their opponents by employing subtle—or not so subtle—forms of proselytizing,* persecution, ridicule or patient example in order to move them along the spectrum from theism to atheism—with its attendant shades of meaning—or in the opposite direction, as the case may be.

I am not opting for a bland and irenic indifference when tolerance and respect for divergent experiences is suggested. Nor am I implying that there are no valid grounds for labeling certain behaviors pathological. Delusion may crop up in religious matters as surely as it does in politics or academe or wherever human reality-testing falters. Psychopathology* is too broad a field—and much too controversial—to linger over the idea that some persons may be out of touch with their own experiencing.[54] It is also taken for granted that aberrations do not fairly represent the phenomenon of any specific human activity, religious or otherwise. We gain little insight if we take as representative of their fields the stereotypical religious fanatic, the mad scientist or the power-crazed politician.

It has not been my intention to propose that it makes no difference what a person believes. Stated thus abstractly it runs the risk of demeaning the importance of those values and experiences which most immediately and convincingly express who we are as persons. Rather my goal has been to emphasize the necessary qualities of humility, respect and uncertainty that are as much a part of the quest for meaning and value as are our deepest convictions and commitments.

I usually ask my students in class if they find the Hindu attitude toward the sacred cow[55] to be comprehensible to them. The majority conviction is that it is bizarre and a total inversion of common sense values. If human life is paramount, they reason, cows should be slaughtered to provide food.

The presumption is that "they" are foolish whereas "we" are enlightened. When I point out that a Hindu finds the American mania for big cars and super highways to be an inversion of values, there is generally a pause. Hindus point out that cows give milk, fertilizer and fuel as well as birthing oxen for farm labor. They serve many useful functions, not the least of which is an emphasis on spiritual values. Our sacred cow, a Hindu might counter, is the car, a monster that pollutes the environment, uses up precious fossil fuels and is expensive to run and maintain. They know the statistics that show that more Americans are killed or maimed in auto accidents each year than have been killed in any war in our history. Convenience, not human life, is our priority, or else our cars would be smaller, slower, cheaper and safer.

The point is clear, I hope. A custom or belief may strike us as strange or downright stupid if we are unwilling to see things from a different perspective and to admit that we may ourselves have become accustomed to practices that are not very rational just because they are common. We oftentimes have to attempt to approach other myths with lessened defenses and without a preconceived sense of the inherent superiority of what our own cultural and religious myths stress. We need not cease to value our own myth when we sensitively study another understanding of reality. We may well discover insights, values and wisdom that broaden our viewpoint, make us less intolerant and more attuned to the profundity of human existence. In the bargain we may return to the wellsprings of our own myths as more knowledgeable and committed even as we are more sensitive and open to alternative myths. There are few things in life of which we are infallibly certain, but one absolute fact is this: the sign of a truly ignorant person is the rejection of that which one does not understand. To understand even a bit better the allegiance given to various religious myths by millions of persons is to understand a bit more clearly the questions that have fascinated human beings throughout history and, by implication, to know ourselves a bit more accurately.

A few towns away from where I teach there has been another in a series of arsons that have left many Cambodian immigrants homeless. Police say the "haters" are threatened by persons different from themselves and they fear change in their insular world. Even as these bigots are acting like Nazi storm troopers they likely flatter themselves that they are "true" Americans. Ignorance can be a very dangerous thing.

Glossary

Atrophy is a wasting away, a diminution.

The **Enlightenment** was an 18th century philosophical movement that stressed critical reasoning and which challenged all institutions and teachings based on authority or tradition.

Proselytizing is attempting to convert someone to another belief.

Psychopathology is that area of psychology that studies mental illness or antisocial behavior.

Study Questions

1. Why is it so difficult to understand our own experience?

2. Can you prove your own existence or that your parents love you? What does this suggest about our ability to empirically validate most choices we make?

3. What does this chapter suggest about the possibility of one world religion, culture or language?

4. Why do arguments for and against God's existence rarely lead us to change our position?

5. Read Sigmund Freud's *The Future of an Illusion*. Describe how he interprets religious beliefs.

6. Write about your own trip abroad or interview someone who has visited or lived in another country. Discuss the difference in myth you detect.

Further Reading

1. James Cone, *For My People* (Maryknoll: Orbis, 1984).

2. Peter Kelly, *Searching for Truth* (Cleveland: Collins, 1978).

3. Jacob Needleman, *Lost Christianity* (New York: Bantam, 1982).

4. Rosemary Ruether and Eleanor McLaughlin, eds., *Women of Spirit* (New York: Simon and Schuster, 1979).

5. Joachim Wach, *Types of Religious Experience* (Chicago: University of Chicago Press, 1972).

5.

The Critical Analysis of Myths

There are a number of show-biz psychologists who make the rounds of talk-shows and speak with firm voice and steady eye about the most inane clues to human behavior. The more gullible viewer is wont to absorb as truth unassailable the connection between the color of one's sofa and the "real" person. Still others, presumably intelligent and sophisticated individuals, breathlessly talk of the profound insights into self gained by spending a weekend on a hard chair and being verbally abused by the latest guru of the self-awareness cult. Other individuals, desperate to look like models without having to sacrifice beer and pizza, reject elementary knowledge of nutrition and buy the latest diet book that guarantees to effortlessly turn the beast into a beauty.

All of these examples are simply variations on the old shell game and are predicated on the gamble that many persons are notoriously resistant to using their common sense or to thinking for themselves. If an "authority" speaks, especially when the proper letters appear after the name, many persons take as truth what may be merely opinion, wishful thinking or blatant nonsense. They prefer to be led rather than to explore, to be given answers rather than to raise questions. Nowhere is this more dangerous than in matters of religion since religion has the awesome potential of eliciting a total response from the believer and of offering an ultimate explanation for all human striving.

How are we to be sure that a religious myth is worthy of our belief and commitment? No simple answer is forthcoming for two reasons.

1. The viability or vitality of a religious myth is often able to be judged only in retrospect. In other words, all of the great religions of the world were probably considered impractical in their inception and certainly major religious figures found their vision met great opposition when they attempted to communicate it to others. Buddha, Moses, Zoroaster,* Jesus, Muhammed and others were accused of everything from megalomania* to demonic possession. This is understandable since they ruptured the existing paradigm by which their societies had lived and appealed to a reordering of reality that involved tremendous personal risk on the part of the listener. Why some responded wholeheartedly and others resisted vehemently takes us into the gray area between reason and faith. The English Catholic author, Ronald Knox, once asked a scholar who had written a very balanced and sensitive history of the Catholic Church why he had not become a Catholic himself. To which the historian replied: "To understand is not to believe."

It is too simple to reduce faith to a matter of autosuggestion,[56] although that may well be an element present in some or many religious conversions, nor, on the other hand, to strenuously insist that faith is a gift that overwhelms the individual and allows no rejection.[57] The former position insists there is no God possible of drawing forth a faith response, whereas the latter judges a lack of faith to be evidence of pride or malice.

We have noted that experience posits a searcher and an object of one's search, a traveler and a destination, even as we have allowed for the possibility of detours or dead ends. If God or Ultimate Reality exists, "He/She or It" can only be responded to within our human experience and by carefully interpreting the guideposts along the road that is our own life unfolding. It is better to avoid talk of a "leap" of faith, but rather to speak of a "risk" of faith. It would be demeaning to suggest that belief requires that we take leave of our reason; better to say that our reason and experience lead us to the point where we risk defining ourselves in a broader context, within a new relationship. Faith or enlightenment that is coercive is unworthy of either God or us. If there is a God or Absolute who beckons, there must be a freely given response from the searcher.

When the followers of the Buddha, the Christ and Muhammed responded in faith to their respective visions and persons it was on the basis of risk undergirded with certainty, a reflection of the cry of the father whose son was cured: "I do believe. Help my unbelief!" (Mark 9:25). There was a resonance within the depths of each mature convert, a convergence of giver and receiver that enlightened and vivified the experience of each believer. The object of faith was firmly and surely part of the fabric of a living experience:

> Moreover, the genuinely religious man knows that the demand for a proof which will coerce the self through sheer necessity ... is actually the most subtle form of asking for a sign and of trying to achieve the religious relationship in a manner which avoids decision and risk.[58]

The object of religious experience then must not only be intellectually grasped but grasped within the flux of each person's experiences. Even when one is open to broadening one's experience, to responding to the Beyond within, there is no way of avoiding the risk and complexity of one's own personal evaluation. "Are you the one who is to come, or have we got to wait for someone else?" (Matthew 11:3) indicates that faith or enlightenment does not relieve the searcher from the task of discernment. Obviously one major criterion for deciding was the attractiveness of the message shared. How the religious figure acted was a confirmation of what he said and the example given had to have tremendous impact. Another vital ingredient in the faith response was that subtle but yet concrete quality called "charisma."[59]

The charismatic personality, in sheer presence, words and actions, is able to trigger a response in the hearers, a response which leads to an act of faith in who he is or what she says. Nonetheless, the object of one's religious experience is totally and maturely accepted only when the individual completes the experiential process of observing, evaluating, judging, and accepting. It is only by looking back in honest reflection on one's life and by situating one's faith within the fullest expression of one's total life experience that a judgment about one's faith response is possible.

2. Closely connected, and really an integral part of the response of faith, is the process of self-understanding. It is sometimes reasonably justifiable to judge that certain persons are acting from motives different from those of which they are conscious. Some individuals marry to get away from an unhappy home life; some persons turn to religion because they are insecure and frightened; others choose certain professions to compensate for a sense of inadequacy. These behavior patterns may appear obvious to an astute observer but will be rejected as ludicrous by the person making the choice. Why is this so?

At the risk of oversimplification, the greatest mystery we will encounter in life is ourselves. This is not to say that we are totally unaware of our true motives but rather that we become so familiar with our thought and behavior patterns that only an observer may see what is no longer obvious to ourselves. Psychological literature is replete with terms like incongruence*, avoidance mechanisms, inappropriate responses, repression and the like to make a case for this position.

Does this mean that we are condemned to float through life like amorphous blobs resembling plastic jet-setters who exchange personalities along with current fads and costumes? Hardly. I am saying that the most intelligent and the most sophisticated person, no less than the uninformed or the naive, needs feedback from others in order to stay in touch with one's own experience and one's truest motives. Call one a friend, a confidant or a significant other, the point is that we need others we can trust and respect to act as sounding boards. These complements to ourselves serve to keep us in touch with our depths, our honest perspectives and our real choices. To the ex·ent that we know ourselves we can trust our experience and the choices that flow from that experience.

In religious matters it may well entail hearing attentively the questions put to us by ourselves and others. Am I using religion as a crutch to avoid dealing with any fears and uncertainties? Am I professing atheism because I dread going beyond my neatly constructed little world of facts? Is my agnosticism sincere or is it a matter of intellectual laziness or fashionable posturing?

We may, through introspection, reach a reasonable judgment that we can rely on and act on accordingly. In other cases we may need another to give us insights, raise questions, play devil's advocate. Such sharing can be invaluable in casting light on hidden motives or in reinforcing our conviction that we are persons of integrity acting on our most valid insights. All of which is to say that we can never be absolutely certain that we may not be playing games with ourselves but that we do trust our experience because we have made every reasonable effort to follow Socrates' maxim: "The unexamined life is not worth living."

In matters of self-knowledge, as in religious matters, many persons seek "the answer" to unraveling the mystery. They can use a personality theory or a theoretical construct as a substitute for their own search. I remember hearing a young psychiatrist relating his personal journey from the printed page to the real world. He had been practicing a short time in Manhattan when he was drafted and sent to an army base in Mississippi. In a matter of a few weeks it became painfully obvious that his most cherished beliefs about human personality did not "fit." He slowly began to see that his professors had taught *one* approach as *the* approach to helping people. It worked fine with middle-class, urban and articulate patients but was inappropriate with rural, semi-literate and poor persons. He then began to take classes at local colleges and to be introduced to other personality theorists. Gradually he developed an eclectic* approach to helping people, convinced that human personality was too complex and unpredictable to be forced into the narrow confines of any single approach. He now sees his role as guide, not at authority, as one who seeks to aid others in understanding their own experience and in taking responsibility for their own lives. Although he does not hesitate to state his viewpoints when asked, he is most careful not to pass off his personal convictions as objective truth. He supports his clients in the process of elucidating their own convictions.

We are not condemned to go through life playing "The Newlywed Game" by constantly second-guessing ourselves and others. We have every reason to trust our experience if we have been self-reflective and simultaneously open to the valid insights of others. No one is going to give us self-awareness or faith. That is simply to turn over responsibility to others and live their experience vicariously. In the end we must be willing to take the risk of trusting our own informed experience. We may turn out to be mistaken and we may entertain doubts, but this should not frighten us. Doubt may well be the purifying process that returns us again and again to our deepest convictions and that forces us to be honest to ourselves and to our object of faith.

How then are we "sure" of our religious beliefs? We are certain if they are anchored in our experience, that complex, profound and ongoing process that reflects our self-awareness and our openness to the experiences and insights of others. Eventually the choice is mine, just as all the major decisions in life are mine. To be afraid to trust our experience because we may be wrong is to opt for *rigor mortis*, a predictable but hardly exciting condition.

All well and good, you might say, but are there any criteria I can employ for deepening my own self-awareness in the religious dimension of experience? Keeping in mind that different schools of psychology emphasize various qualities in constructing personality theory, we may answer affirmatively and state that only a mature person is capable of a mature religious experience. There are certain characteristics, culled from clinical experience and observation, that may be expected to help us distinguish the mature from the immature religious experience.[60] We can usefully put certain questions to ourselves about our religious attitudes which may serve as a corrective to self-deception:

1. Is my religious perspective *hierarchical,* that is am I able to perceive that certain beliefs, customs or practices are less important than others within the totality of my religious experience? What an individual or a group singles out as a major focus for concern is indicative of a religious attitude that is either stifling or flexible. There is something very disconcerting about religious persons who will become enraged at the presence of a massage parlor in their neighborhood and yet be completely oblivious to the obscenity of slums through which they drive to work. Certain Catholics will insist on viewing changes in fasting laws, liturgical expression or the

clothing of priests and sisters as being on the same level with belief in the sacraments or the divinity of Christ. The tendency to overemphasize minor concerns and neglect more important ones; the inability to perceive the historical circumstances that may no longer suffice to perpetuate certain customs, or an exaggerated preoccupation with peripheral ethical issues (*e.g.*, drinking or gambling) are clues to an uncritical and unreflective religious position. The dangers of self-righteousness and intolerance are very real.

2. Am I *consistent* in my attitudes and convictions such that there is a comprehensiveness within my religious experience? An individual who vehemently opposes abortion and yet favors capital punishment or an aggressive military policy may well have a very confused understanding of human life in all forms. As an editor of a science journal noted, one's position, pro or con, on abortion is logically joined to one's position on euthanasia since they are both concerned with the quality of life itself at opposite ends of the life spectrum. We all know persons who rant about welfare fraud but think nothing of buying a stolen stereo from a friend who has "connections." There are many examples possible but it should be clear that an individual who reacts to specific issues with heated emotion rather than basing judgments on consistent principles will evidence a very distorted understanding of the relationship to the object of one's religious experience.[61]

3. Is my religious perspective *developmental*, allowing for change and adjustment as my own experience deepens and expands? I have met a great number of adults who will say, "I was taught that. . ." and fall back on a position that reflects an unquestioning acceptance of childhood teachings that are not suitable for an adult intelligence. Others, especially in times of sorrow or distress, will complain that "God is punishing me" or "He didn't grant my request when I have been praying so long." Such conceptualizations of God as a cosmic policeman or a celestial Santa Claus reveal little movement away from a God of childish fantasy towards a God of mystery and hidden presence. As we move from childhood into adulthood we learn to re-evaluate our options and to deal with a world of complexity and ambiguity. The black and white certitudes of youth are fit only for children who have yet to learn that idealism untempered by realism leads to

fanaticism. If there are traces of fantasy, superstition or magic in my practices there is a strong indication that my religious development is arrested at a stage inappropriate for an adult.[62] How we think about God may reveal more about our own personal development than we may be aware.

4. Does my religious conviction lead me to be *tolerant* or does my religious experience cause me to reject the beliefs of others? Am I able to respect the honest journey of another whose language or beliefs may differ from mine or am I certain that my religious experience is universally valid for everyone? History is replete with horrible examples of torture and bloodshed perpetrated by so-called "true believers" upon others whose conscience would not permit forsaking their deepest convictions. A rather controversial public figure recently admitted that even her best and most caring friends would burn in hell if they were not Christians. What are we to make of bumper stickers proclaiming "Kill a queer (or commie) for Christ?" By what warped reasoning does the Prince of Peace become transformed into a brutal Aztec deity? Examples are to be found in every religious tradition, indicating the perverse human tendency to create and mutate God in our own image and likeness.

If our religious life is not developmental there will inevitably develop intolerance of other religious positions. Instead of gratitude for one's faith and a commitment to ultimate reality that speaks most fully to us, some persons and groups are compelled to proselytize to the point of creating resentment and disdain for religion.

A student of mine told me about an interesting experience she had last summer. She and her boyfriend were going for ice cream at a shore resort when they came upon a motorcycle accident. They and others ran over to assist the victim. Out of the crowd stepped a man with some religious material and he attempted to force it on them. When they said they were not interested he informed them they were both doomed to hell. My student was amazed at this man's assumption that no other religious belief could possibly be satisfying and meaningful.

A long-standing history of confusion and scandal has been the responsibility of Christian missionaries who penetrated American Indian reservations, African lands and Asian nations. So much energy was expended trying to entice Christians of other denominations into other folds that bigotry was communicated along with baptism.[63]

It is small comfort to Christians to know that Moslems slew Buddhists and Hindus when they invaded India in the 12th century nor that Confucianism, Taoism and Shintoism have sought to establish predominance over their rivals at various points in time. It is hardly edifying in our own day to walk through a shopping mall and observe Moonies and Hare Krishna members berating each other for being in error.

It is safe to assume that whenever a religious conviction leads a person to deride or attack others we are witnessing both intense insecurity and insufferable arrogance. To be tolerant is not to be indifferent but to realize that one's own deepest conviction should not allow the erroneous conclusion that God is not present in other cultures and religions in ways amenable to their unique history. Dialogue, not confrontation, is the approach to differing experiences of religion. If smug self-assurance and condescending appraisals of other religious positions are part of our religious expression, then the object of our commitment is communicated as an obstacle to human personhood. Delusions of grandeur in religious matters is no less serious a condition than other expressions of psychological disturbance. Such a mind-set provides every indication that this "true believer"[64] is inhabiting a world created by personal unresolved needs rather than relating to the Other who calls us all into fullest being and responsible freedom.

5. Is my religious experience *integral,* that is, does it admit of a flexibility that is able to mesh my faith stand with knowledge from other disciplines? If the need for meaning, which a religious myth fulfills, is satisfied at the expense of my desire to know and to critically reflect, it is a precarious faith protected by selective ignorance. If one's religious attitude forces one to regress to an earlier, unreflective stage of creating an untroubled world of certitude, oblivious of the messiness of adult existence, it can be judged that religion in this person is actually injurious to human consciousness.

When I was a high school teacher I once granted a request from two college students, who were missionaries for their Church, to speak to a very bright class. During their presentation it became all too clear that many of their beliefs not only flew in the face of scientific knowledge but even of common sense. One rather strange position put forward was that the American Indians would turn into white persons when the entire population converted to their denomination. Apart from the blatant racism (which they insisted was justified by God's revelation) my students were shocked at their ignorance of even basic genetics. The young missionaries simply replied, "If it comes to a conflict between science and religion, I choose to follow my faith."

Such a placid vision of reality may have kept conflicts at bay, but it must sadly be said that such an idyllic existence made them the intellectual equals of some obscure tribe in the Amazon jungle:

> Psychotherapists of various schools often refer, in a variety of metaphors, to a basic need to outgrow and transfigure the stories that have shaped personal identity. Such transformation sometimes occur only along with tumultuous periods of conflict and prolonged emptiness and depression. What was once meaningful may no longer appear to be so, simply because one's horizons have expanded at the suggestion of some other urge than the sheer will to stable meaning.[65]

It may safely be judged that a religious position that purposely ignores the "information explosion" and rejects any need to constantly balance what I know with what I believe can only be maintained within a ghetto, physical or psychological. The mature religious experience is not undermined by the challenge of new insights and hypotheses emanating from the natural sciences, psychology, sociology or medicine. Because one apprehends life as an ongoing process of fitting the bits and pieces of knowledge and belief into a coherent whole, the mature religious person is capable of critically evaluating one's own religious myth even as one learns to separate supposition from tentative fact in other areas of knowledge.[66] Sometimes our most basic religious values will serve as a corrective to extreme or dangerous trends in the social or physical sciences (*e.g.* genetic engineering; racist or sexist social theory, *etc.*) whereas we will also be open to re-evaluating or updating certain religious positions when valid information is presented (*e.g.* anthropological datings; personality and motivation studies, *etc.*).

If, as Jesus said, "The truth will make you free" (John 8:32), then a vital religious myth is open to full and free dialogue with all other areas of life. Fear of exploring certain areas of knowledge lest my "faith be shaken" is a clue to a religious position that will inevitably fail to sustain us during a lifetime of experiencing. Even a genius like Isaac Newton (1642-1727) is said to have avoided certain investigations because he foresaw a threat to central Christian beliefs.[67]

6. Is my religious experience *dynamic*, as indicated by actions consistent with my professed convictions? Psychologists tell us that we tend to externalize our internal attitudes when they are strongly held. In other words, behavior flows from belief, and my decisions and speech give a clear indication of what I truly hold.

Studies on racial prejudice indicate that among many persons with strong religious sentiments there is often a high degree of intolerance. A careful analysis indicates that in such persons their religion is closely tied to an institution, very exclusionist and self-centered. The Church becomes the object of faith rather than the vehicle pointing beyond itself to God.[68] In other words, the divergence between professed beliefs and contradictory behavior indicates these persons are acting out of personal insecurity rather than relating in an enlightened and challenging manner to the object of their faith. A religious position that does not call one to change unethical patterns of behavior or that does not discomfit one who speaks of the unity of humankind while the person harbors hatred of minorities is unworthy of the name.

A conviction eventuates in specific choices and attitudes; an idea or whimsy remains vague and unfocused if it is not seriously held by the individual. The destructive patterns of slavery, warfare, torture and deception that have been a part of human history, regardless of religious and cultural differences, indicate that many persons fail to see the implications that follow from stated positions.

Religious experience, if it is vital and realistic, is never just a matter of orthodox doctrinal statements, liturgical precision or eloquent rhetoric. If religion is truly a part of a person's life it leads to behavior that is congruent with one's personal beliefs. If the behavior contradicts what one claims to believe, it is a fair assertion that one says what one knows but has no real understanding of what one says. The basis for all hypocrisy is lip service paid to ideals that are never put into practice because they are theoretical positions and not genuine existential choices.[69]

The sociologist of religion, Joachim Wach, states, "Religious experience is a total response of the total being to what is apprehended as ultimate reality. That is, we are involved not exclusively with our mind, our affections or our will, but as integral persons."[70]

Religion is not a detached philosophy of life but a way of being present to life. If religion is unrelated to the practical consequences of daily existence there is every likelihood that religious experience in that instance is not a living conviction but a moribund convention.

It may be added that a sense of humor is an important ingredient in religious experience. Beyond the personal difficulty I have always had in seeing any logical connection between pursed lips, a dour visage and religious experience, history reveals that there has always been a strong Dionysian[71] element in all forms of religion. Religion has always claimed to usher its adherents into a realm beyond the mundane and pedestrian reality of our daily concerns. That such an experience of ultimate reality or the presence of God is awesome and humbling, perhaps terrifying, there is no doubt. And yet there is an element of humor in the quest of limited and fallible human beings seeking to reach the source of infinite Being.

Perhaps St. Theresa of Avila realized this point when, during a very difficult time in her life, she prayed to God, "If this is the way you treat your friends, I really pity your enemies." Somewhere between hackneyed expressions like "The Man Upstairs" that tend to liken God to an absentee landlord and "The Great Scorekeeper in the Sky" which makes God into a combination umpire and truant officer, there is a healthy blend of reverence and relaxation. If we learn not to take ourselves too seriously as we ask serious questions, we may find our religious experience allows for greater tolerance of other viewpoints even as it opens us to a deepening sense of awe and wonder at the presence of God or ultimate reality within our own lives.

We may conclude by evaluating the subjective pole of religious experience as trustworthy if it opens us to life, leads to a more tolerant, grateful and respectful attitude towards ourselves and others, is open to insights and correctives from other persons and other areas of knowledge, is flexible and capable of critical and ongoing re-evaluation, opening and expanding our horizons.

Finally a sense of humor cautions us from taking ourselves too seriously and keeps us vitally attuned to the object of our belief, the source of surprise, awe and unpredictable possibilities. We need not hesitate to act confidently in the religious dimension of experience when we have met the criteria of reasonable self-knowledge required of every mature person in all aspects of our living. The Other who invites us to be completed in our relationship with Him does so on the basis of our being complete within ourselves.

Summary

Sociologists tell us that there are many ways of being human depending on the social support given to various views of reality.[72] Human beings share a common biological inheritance, obviously, but the development of the cerebral cortex, the employment of language and ritual, and the varied artistic expressions of the human race suggest that we are better defined as a "symbol maker" than as a "rational animal." The myriad ways in which inquisitive human beings experience reality cautions us against limiting knowledge (what people take to be true) to only one epistemology or to only our familiar paradigms.

I once taught an undergraduate class in the psychology of religion and was surprised to find heightened interest in the analysis of consciousness expansion through meditation, right-hemisphere functioning, mysticism, *etc*. This particular class included a number of serious practitioners of various forms of Oriental martial arts and they were eager to learn the history and rationale for many of their practices. They had employed what the Buddhists called "focused attention" or "singlemindedness" and were very disposed to view other reality-constructs in an open-minded manner. All of them saw the value of meditation and could appreciate the focus of Buddhist goals.

Another student in the same class was a Chinese engineering student who confessed to me that she had little knowledge of her Buddhist roots and had, in fact, been too embarrassed to study her religion because it was "impractical."

By the end of the course she expressed a longing to study Buddhism anew and judged that she had written her religion off because she was relying on epistemologies appropriate to science to deal with more personal questions.

It seems of vital importance that we understand the ways in which our personal experience is molded even as we rely on it and trust it as the only means we possess for dealing with reality. Our experience is vital and trustworthy when it is informed by honest self-reflection and by openness to the insights and experiences of others. The process of sifting and evaluating is co-terminal with life itself. Openness to life is simultaneously openness to growth and change, unless we move away from ourselves as the center of our experiencing and allow ourselves to be subsumed under one or another authoritarian epistemology. We then make someone else's mistake instead of taking the risk of humbly but critically owning our personal experience.

In the religious dimension of experience only an informed and reflective faith position is worthy of a mature individual. Defensive reactions against valid criticism or a lack of willingness to analyze our motivations are signs of an overriding desire for security and certitude at the expense of what may be a more tenuous but much more vital religious myth:

> Is a religion coming to birth in our time? It could be. What seems to be occurring is a phenomenon we might call "passing over," passing over from one culture to another, from one way of life to another. Passing over is a shifting of standpoint, a going over to the standpoint of another culture, another way of life, another religion. It is followed by an equal and opposite process we might call "coming back," coming back with new insight to one's own culture, one's own way of life, one's own religion.[73]

Socialization is a risky enterprise.[74] It alleviates the need to reinvent the wheel every generation by providing a framework of meaning into which each person is born. Marshall MacLuhan once said that "each generation stands on the shoulders of the ones preceding it," and so we have an immediate vehicle for structuring our potential and for passing on the accumulated experiences of our predecessors. Society, in sociological parlance, holds chaos at bay by providing the tools for interpreting the complex world around us.

Socialization, however, can subtly insinuate a disregard for other cultural evolutions and lead to the unwarranted assumption that what is different is inferior or wrong. Our personally introjected social beliefs may lead to the parochial position of insisting that our familiar experience must necessarily be the criterion for all human experience. In this instance we approach other cultures and religions, if at all, not to observe and to learn but to confront and belittle. I remember hearing an American mercenary, who was fighting in support of the white regime in Rhodesia,* justifying his position by an appeal to "maintaining a Western way of life." He explained, in all seriousness, that you could not find a decent chocolate bar in Asia nor a good hamburger in Africa. Presumably he was fighting to make tooth decay and indigestion the inalienable rights of all people. So much for the broadening experience of world travel.

When we speak of studying other myths or "passing over" to other religions and cultures there is no need to turn our back on our own myths.

We explore to deepen our awareness of the differing approaches to reality and to understand why other myths speak to other cultures. In the undertaking we may come to appreciate and comprehend our own myth more deeply and to inculcate awe for the wondrous ingenuity and adaptability of all searching human beings as they create a world of meaning. Commitment based on knowledge of alternative myths is far more secure than allegiance predicated on cultural or religious dogmatism.[75]

Glossary

Eclectic means the mixing or combining of various sources or ideas to form a position or viewpoint.

Incongruence in psychology means that there is a contradiction between what one says and what one does.

Megalomania is a condition of fantasizing great wealth, power or importance.

Rhodesia, a former British colony, is now the African nation of Zimbabwe.

Zoroaster, also called **Zarathustra**, was the sixth century B.C. founder of a dualistic religion in Persia. There was a God of light and a God of darkness who contended for mastery of the universe and control of human destiny.

Study Questions

1. How do you explain the prejudice among so many churchgoers? Is religion bad for our mental health?

2. How do the criteria presented in this chapter apply to your own religious attitudes?

3. Describe your present understanding of God and compare it to ten years ago. Has there been a change? In what ways?

4. What does the statement: "To know one religion is to know none" mean to you?

5. Research the mass murders associated with cult leader Jim Jones. Discuss what led people to follow him.

6. Discuss with a classmate or a teacher from another country how they react to hearing America referred to as "the best country in the world."

Further Reading

1. Gordon Allport, *The Individual and his Religion* (New York: Macmillan, 1964)

2. Mircea Eliade, *The Sacred and the Profane* trans. Willard R. Trask, (New York: Harper, 1961).

3. Lawrence LeShan, *Alternate Realities* (New York: Ballantine, 1977).

4. Edward Stevens, *The Religion Game, American Style* (New York: Paulist, 1976).

6.

Three Universal Religious Myths

On what basis does one decide to treat only three religions and to deal with others in a peripheral way at most? It should be made clear from the outset that there is no implication that Buddhism, Christianity and Islam are "better" myths than Judaism, Hinduism, Confucianism, Taoism, Shintoism or native religions, although their adherents may well dispute such a disclaimer.

These three religions are the focus of our study for two reasons:

1. They are historical in a particular way, having originated with a person whose history is fairly accessible to us and who claimed to speak with authority and to offer a new vision of reality. Judaism is most assuredly an historical religion, tracing its beginnings to Abraham, the father of faith. The calling of Abraham is recorded in Genesis 12 wherein God establishes a special covenant (solemn pact) with Abraham and his descendents.

Some scholars, however, doubt the historicity of the Biblical patriarchs, although their names and ways of life were consonant with the history of the Fertile Crescent* at the beginning of the second millennium B.C. Other scholars would assign the determining shape of Israelite religion to Moses who lived perhaps some 600 years after Abraham. The religion of Israel took a more formal turn when David became the first effective king of his nation. The role of the prophets added yet another dimension to Jewish religion, all of which is to say that Judaism, which has always been con-

59

cerned with God's activity in history, sees the covenant as being received by the nation through a number of individuals.

Hinduism, perhaps the oldest and most complex of all the world's religions, is traced by comparative religionists, at least in certain forms and themes, to the third millennium B.C. Hindus distinguish between *shruti* or the Scriptures handed down by God Himself and *smirti* which are of divine origin but have been transmitted through human beings. Hindus call their religion *sanatana dharma* or "eternal religion" and believe it has always existed. Although there have been major figures in the development of Hinduism, no historical personage is designated the founder of this religion.

The religions of China, Confucianism and Taoism, are not concerned with historical roots in the same way Western religions are. Both religions are interwoven into the total philosophy of the Chinese *people* and reflect an earlier period of syncretistic development.

The founder of Taoism is traditionally thought to be Lao-tzu who is purported to have lived in the sixth century B.C. Little is known about him and many scholars doubt that he actually existed, being perhaps a compilation of a number of persons. The book that Lao-tzu is supposed to have written is the *Tao Te Ching,* "The Classic of the Way and Its Power or Virtue." It has been translated more times than any other book in the world except the Bible and is a major source of Chinese thought.

Kung Fu-tsu, known to history as Confucius, was a contemporary of the legendary Lao-tzu and of the Buddha, born in 551 B.C. His genius was as a collator of traditional ethical practices which Confucius updated and applied to political theory and personal and social goals. The *Analects* are ascribed to Confucius and have had enormous influence in China for almost 25 centuries.

Neither Confucianism nor Taoism were originally seen as religions. They had no priesthood, no sacred writings viewed as revealed, no asceticism or monasticism and no doctrine of an afterlife. There were later cultic developments in both religions—or philosophies—but neither Confucius nor Lao-tzu considered themselves religious founders.

In Japan the indigenous religion is Shinto, which means "The Way of the Gods." Like Hinduism it embraces a variety of practices and beliefs, and Shintoism appears to have evolved from a nationalistic mythology. Japan and the Japanese people are traced to the appearance of the gods "in the beginning." The major Shinto scriptures *Kojiki*, "Records of Ancient Matters" and *Nihongi*, "The Japanese Chronicles" date from the eighth century A.D. and are not held to be revealed.

The native religions of the American Indians and of African peoples tend to be ahistorical in their inception and to rely on "carriers" or oral transmitters rather than on written scriptures to communicate their religious beliefs. Like Hinduism, native American and African religions trace their origins into the dim recesses of creation and believe there is a special and timeless relationship between God and the tribe.

2. They are universal in conception and have all engaged in missionary activity to bring their message to other cultures.

Within Judaism there have been brief periods of missionary endeavor but the belief of the Jews as the "Chosen People" carries the conviction that the special covenant exists only between God and this people. Even though Jews maintain that all sincere persons can be saved by following their conscience, Judaism is intrinsically related to a Promised Land and a Chosen People, thus limiting its universal appeal.

Hinduism has manifested little interest in proselytizing other peoples and tends to be limited to the Indian subcontinent and to groups of expatriates in communities scattered throughout the world. Because of the Hindu belief that "Truth is one, but man calls it by many names," there has been a remarkable tolerance of other religions and other understandings of Ultimate Reality. Hinduism is and will be, for any number of reasons, the religion of India but not of the world.

Confucianism and Taoism arose to meet specific needs within Chinese culture and have never had great appeal to other societies except in terms of the ethical simplicity of their respective philosophies. Although Confucianism influenced Japanese constitutional reform and Taoism's impact on Buddhism eventuated in Zen, neither religion was communicated as requiring adherence exclusive of other religions.

Shinto is really the national religion of Japan and is intrinsically related to the geography and history of a single people. Shinto, a tribal religion centered in national traditions which are symbolized in the person of the Emperor, is by nature limited in its appeal outside of Japan.

American Indian and African religions are also tribal and have never made a pretense of appealing to other tribes or religions. Both native religions make allowance for each tribe and culture having its own sacred traditions and conceptions of God, and it is unthinkable that there exists a revelation or a path to enlightenment which is the common heritage of all of us.

The rationale for selecting only three out of the many religious myths that have been part of human history does not deny the appeal, beauty and value of other myths. In an age of ecological destruction there is an invaluable and urgent lesson to be learned from the respect for nature and the view of humans as tenants on the earth long held by the native religions of North America, Africa and Asia.

As well, the broad tolerance for other traditions reflective of American Indian, African and Hindu religion is a needed corrective to much of the religious and nationalistic chauvinism* that perpetuates disdain and ignorance of differing reality systems.

Judaism is truly the mother religion of both Christianity and Islam, neither one of which makes sense nor could have prospered in isolation from the Jewish faith. The basis of the prophetic tradition for a developed sense of social justice in Western society needs no defense, and the central place of the Jewish Bible in expressing humankind's highest aspirations is beyond dispute.

To focus our attention on Christianity and Islam is not to neglect Judaism, reference to which will be made at appropriate points. Likewise Buddhism cannot be understood apart from the richness of Indian religious thought as expressed in Hinduism. The very real contributions made to

Buddhism as it encountered Confucianism, Taoism and Shintoism may also be noted. The major emphasis upon the Buddha, the Christ and Muhammed allows us to enter the shared experience of an historical figure who claimed to bring a message that could answer everyone's need for purpose and meaning. If we approach these great persons with respect it is not because we judge other myths to be less worthy of our attention and the fidelity of other believers. Our journey is by no means the only possible path to follow.[76]

Glossary

The **Fertile Crescent** was a great arc of land stretching for some 1,200 miles from Mesopotamia (present day Iraq and Iran) to Egypt. It was dominated by two river systems, the Tigris and Euphrates in Mesopotamia and the Nile in Egypt.

Chauvinism is the belief in the superiority of one's group.

Study Questions

1. Why are Christianity and Islam called the "daughter religions" of Judaism?

2. Why could native religions in America, Africa or Australia never become universal religions?

3. Speculate on why the three great monotheistic religions of Judaism, Christianity and Islam all originated within the Fertile Crescent.

4. Study Chinese family structure and explain why celibacy has no meaning in this tradition.

5. Investigate the role of the Japanese emperor in Shintoism. Why is Shintoism not "exportable" to other nations?

6. Research the life of Confucius. In what ways did he shape Chinese culture for over a thousand years?

Further Reading

1. Denise and John Carmody, *The Story of World Religions* (Mountain View, CA: Mayfield, 1988).

2. Ninian Smart, *The Religious Experience of Mankind* (New York: Charles Scribner's Sons, 1969).

3. Huston Smith, *The Religions of Man* (New York: Perennial Library, 1965).

7.

The Buddha:
The Myth of the Search

Buddhism is a term for a vastly diverse system of beliefs and practices focusing ultimately on the person and teachings of Siddartha Gotama, known to history as The Buddha or "The Enlightened One." Buddhism has its deepest roots in the spiritual soil of India but its greatest impact has been in the development of Asian cultures beyond the Indian subcontinent. The Buddha stands to the East as the Christ does to the West. An awareness of Asian values, only superficially glimpsed by most Westerners, requires at least a basic knowledge of Buddhism, and Buddhism is more clearly seen against the backdrop of Hinduism, the religion it challenged and moved beyond.

It would take us too far afield to explore in depth the complex and rich mosaic of Hindu beliefs, but just as Christianity is beholden to the religious values of Judaism, so too does Buddhism acknowledge a debt to Hindu spirituality.

Hinduism is rooted in the Vedic period, from about 1500 B.C. to 600 B.C. The migration into India of the Aryans ("Noble Folk") led to a grafting on to the animistic* beliefs of the indigenous people of India the religious practices of the Aryans, whose language, religion and social concepts were similar to the Romans and Greeks. Gradually the hymns to the gods, cultic practices and magical rituals passed from oral tradition into the books of the Veda (Knowledge). The composition of these extremely diverse materials was under the guidance of a priestly class or Brahmans.

This period of Indian culture is more accurately referred to as "Brahmanism" rather than as "Hinduism."[77]

In later centuries other sacred literatures evolved, including the highly speculative Upanishads and the more devotional Gitas, the most elaborate epic being the *Bhagavad-Gita*. Alongside the scriptures there flourished various forms of yoga, a discipline concerned with the uniting of the physical, mental and spiritual dimensions of the individual with Saguna Brahma (God with personal attributes) or Nirguna Brahma (Impersonal Ultimate Reality).

Each individual is free to choose the Scriptures one wishes and to follow a form of yoga most conducive to one's own temperament and occupation. Accordingly, union is attainable through various yogas: *jnana* (knowledge), *bhakti* (devotion), *karma* (work) and *raja* (psychological energy).[78]

Such latitude in reaching one's ultimate goal, *atman-Brahman* (the experience of the individual soul united with the ocean of Being or God), has led Hinduism to develop a remarkable tolerance for other religions and for individual initiative.

The Hindu believes there is no distinction between the sacred and the secular spheres—the opposite of Western thought—but that all human beings, through ignorance, confuse the true nature of reality with *maya* or the phenomenal world of appearances. *Maya* is to ultimate reality what a vivid dream is to waking consciousness. It seems real but is actually a product of our mind.

In order to escape *maya* and be released from *samsara* (the transmigration of souls from one existence to another) each individual must follow faithfully the obligations and duties of one's caste. Originally, dating probably from the Aryan period, there were four primary castes: the Brahmans (priests) the Kshatriyas (warriors), the Vaisayas (traders and farmers) and the Sudras (menial workers). Later there developed a fifth caste, the Pariahs or "Untouchables" who were considered nearly subhuman and capable of polluting other castes by their mere presence.[79] The great Hindu pacifist, Mahatma Gandhi, affectionately referred to this caste as *harijan* or "God's people."

The caste system is predicated upon the cosmic law of *karma*, an intricate balance of cause and effect that governs all human activity. There are no neutral thoughts, words or actions, and the law of *karma* determines future existences in various castes. Even God is unable to alter the *karma* of an individual, but, since we are masters of our fate, prayer and devotion may aid the individual in fulfilling caste requirements.[80]

The individual soul (atman) infatuated by *maya* must undergo *samsara* according to the immutable law of *karma* within a given caste. One yearns for *moksha* or release from the cycle of rebirth. In order to avoid confusion, but at the very real risk of distorting a very complex religious tradition, I have not mentioned the Hindu Trinity of Brahma, Vishnu and Shiva, nor have I mentioned the treasury of Hindu scriptures except in passing.[81] A friend of mine who spent a summer in India assured me it is no hyperbole to speak of the "soul of India." The Hindus, he said, are a people "hungry for God." If we pause only briefly to sketch the Hindu myth it is not because it is unimportant but rather that we realize that India is the source of the Buddhist message that was carried beyond its borders.

Siddartha Gotama was born into the Kshatriya caste about 560 B.C., the son of a local chieftain whose territory lay at the foothills of the Himalayan mountains. According to legend, Siddartha's father consulted soothsayers and asked them to plot the course of his infant son's life. If he remains in the world he will become the ruler of all India, they asserted, but he will become the savior of the world if he retires from it. To ensure worldly fame for Siddartha, his father determined to surround him with all the trappings of luxury and pleasure he could provide. Three palaces were built for the young heir, one for each of India's seasons, and great care was taken to anticipate every need of the young man. At age sixteen Siddartha married his cousin Yasodhara and later she gave hem a son, Rahula, on the very day that he encountered The Four Sights.

One day Siddartha desired to tour the royal gardens and this necessitated his father's careful planning to ensure that only young and healthy persons would be encountered. According to the later accounts, written in Sanskrit, Siddartha was aided by heavenly beings in seeing the reality of life. He successively happened upon an old man, a sick man, a dead man and finally a holy man seeking enlightenment. Siddartha returned home, informed his father of his intention of seeking true spiritual peace, departed the palace and left his family. He was 29 years old.[82]

Siddartha sought the meaning of life through the practice of yoga and extreme asceticism, but after seven years he realized that stark asceticism is as much to be avoided as was extreme self-indulgence. Somewhere between these poles lay the middle way.

Siddartha left his forest companions and came to a fig tree and sat down to meditate. Using a technique very similar to raja yoga, Siddartha entered a state of mystical transcendence that gave him the final victory over fear, death, reincarnation and all forms of human limitation. He became the Buddha in this experience and remained in a state of bliss for 49 days. The Buddha, compassionate as well as enlightened, decided to communicate the truth to others, beginning the process of pursuing ultimate reality that continues into our own era. What did the Buddha experience?

Extreme bodily mortification is simply an inversion of physical self—indulgence since either by denial or avowal a preoccupation with the body makes us oblivious to the real problem: ignorance (*avijja*). The Buddha's diagnosis of the human situation centered on the universality of suffering, its cause and its cure. The Buddha realized that sacrifice, rituals, speculations on supernatural orders and philosophical abstractions removed us from undertaking the personal experiential journey towards true enlightenment. Much less was there a need for a specialized priesthood which acted as mediator between us and an unseen reality and which excluded the masses from achieving this esoteric knowledge by employing a defunct Sanskrit language. In short, salvation was an individual and intensely personal undertaking, and while others may support us in the quest, no authority or activity external to ourselves counted for a thing.[83]

The Buddha, concerned to help relieve humankind of its bondage to needless misery, communicated his vision in the Four Noble Truths:

1. The very nature of existence is suffering (*dukka*) and try as we may to convince ourselves otherwise, pain, sorrow and disappointment are the essential characteristics of every life.

2. Suffering is caused by our profound ignorance that: what appears most real and substantial is actually illusory and transient. The phenomenal* world has no more permanence than a puff of smoke and is composed of finite forms subject to decay and dissolution. It is because we are ignorant of the true nature of existence that we are possessed by craving or desire (*tanha*) to grasp whatever ephemeral* entities we pathetically believe will make us happy. We, not some omnipotent deity or some combination of arbitrary cosmic forces, are the cause of our own suffering because we desire to hold what can never be permanent.

3. Incisive and caring diagnostician that he was, the Buddha had no interest in merely deepening the pessimism of his listeners but rather he sought to free them from the wheel of rebirth and from *karma* which makes rebirth inevitable. The fundamental karmic world view of Indian religion was sustained by the Buddha but given a more explicit analysis by the Buddha and his more prominent followers.[84] There is a way out of endless rebirth and it begins with rejecting this most pernicious and fundamental human error: the belief that we have a soul and an individual identity.

> Where Hinduism maintains that the mistaken identity of the self with empirical events, with Samsara, is the ultimate cause of man's predicament, Buddhism declares that a primary cause of man's attachment to existence is his erroneous assumption that he is a continuing self. One proclaims the root of mankind's trouble is the confusion of the self with the world; the other asserts that the problem lies in the conviction that there is a self.[85]

At most we are a combination of physical, mental and sensory forms, what a Western psychologist might call a "stream of consciousness," but we have no soul (*anatta*) and nothing in this existence is permanent. Much less is the soul eternal. What passes from one existence to another based on the desperate craving to prevent dissolution at death, is only a state of awareness not a permanent substance called a "soul." The acceptance of the impermanence and insubstantiality of all things, including a "self," is the prelude to the release from endless rebirth.

4. A form of raja yoga based on the intellectual acceptance of the preceding insights is employed to reach final enlightenment and release known as *Nirvana*.

Nirvana has become a cliché in Western usage and is usually taken to mean "paradise" or "heaven." This is a misunderstanding of the Buddhist expression, for Nirvana is not a place "I" enter but it is rather a condition of enlightenment and the end of illusion. Nirvana is ineffable but it is not mere nothingness or annihilation.[86] The Buddha evidently had no desire to answer clarifying questions about "what" Nirvana is, because this would be an intellectual exercise rather than an experience of the reality he had absorbed. The clearest reply the Buddha provided to balance the positive and negative images in Nirvana is found in the ancient Pali scriptures:

> Verily, there is a realm, where there is neither the solid, nor the fluid, neither heat nor motion, neither this world nor any other world, neither sun nor moon.

> This I call neither arising nor passing away, neither standing still, nor being born, nor dying. There is neither foothold, nor development nor any basis. This is the end of suffering.[87]

If Nirvana was the goal that the Buddha had experienced and which he decided to help all suffering beings attain, it was necessary to provide the means of detachment from the sources of our suffering. The road to Nirvana was mapped out by the Eight-Fold Path. The way was available to everyone regardless of occupation, caste or ethnic origin and Nirvana was the unquestioned right of every sincere searcher for enlightenment.

The Eight-Fold Path is usually presented sequentially and combines ethics and contemplation.

1. *Right Views:* Before one begins a trip it is necessary to have a map, however rudimentary, to envision the end of the travel. Before release from suffering was possible it was necessary to personally accept the Buddha's analysis of reality. The starting point was the intellectual absorption of the

Four Noble Truths. One had to share the Buddha's conviction about life before his formula for redressing suffering made sense.

2. *Right Intention:* Like the heavy smoker who knows the habit is harmful but never does anything concrete to eliminate it, an intellectual acceptance of the Buddhist diagnosis of life requires determination to follow the prescription for the cure. Otherwise, the map is read but the journey is never begun. Step two requires a union of thinking and willing.

3. *Right Speech:* Steps three, four and five are considered to be the ethical basis of the Buddhist myth. Speech is both a medium of communication with others and a technique for concealment. The individual who lies, gossips, slanders or indiscreetly reveals confidences is really involved in a process designed to enhance one's own ego (an illusion) at the expense of others. In demeaning or belittling others the concern is with protecting an impermanent self at the very time we should be most deeply aware that there is no self to protect. Not a general resolve to speak truthfully but a conscious reflection on specific motives and speech patterns is demanded.

4. *Right Action:* Just as impulsive speech can serve to remove us from following our goal, so too can destructive behavior rob us of inward mastery and make us playthings of external circumstances. The precepts have the positive intention of fostering compassion and gentleness even though they are stated as proscriptions: do not kill (devout Buddhists extend this to animals and are vegetarians); do not steal (not only theft but the desire to amass goods is shunned); do not have unlawful intercourse (for the monks and unmarried this meant celibacy and for the married it meant proper control. Dancing, singing, shows and sensual diversion were also to be avoided); do not drink intoxicants (if the mind is clouded by drugs the entire process of seeking enlightenment ceases). Further restrictions were imposed on the monks, not unlike the disciplines specified in Christian monastic orders.

5. *Right Livelihood:* Our modern phrase-makers have coined the word workaholic to refer to an individual possessed by a job and almost neurotically incapable of creative inactivity. The Buddha realized that certain oc-

cupations, by their very nature, required the employment of harmful means to be successful. Opposed to spiritual advancement would be the professions of soldier, butcher, prostitute, slave dealer, brewer, tax collector and certain forms of commerce, among others. The Buddha was concerned that the way one makes a living may well control the quality and direction of one's life.[88]

6. *Right Effort:* The Buddha talked at length of the need to continuously exercise the will "to avoid," "to overcome," "to develop," and "to maintain." By this he meant that temptations had to be avoided, habits to be overcome, virtues to be developed and meritorious conditions maintained:

> Those who follow the way might well follow the example of an ox that marches through the deep mire carrying a heavy load. He is tired, but his steady gaze, looking forward, will never relax until he comes out of the mire, and it is only then he takes a respite. O monks, remember that passion and sin are more than filthy mire, and that you can escape misery only by earnestly and steadily thinking of the Way.[89]

The tedious and constant attention to the effort at hand would gradually become so much a part of the disciple that it would be performed easily, but in the meantime the Buddha exhorted:

> May rather skin, sinews and bones wither away, may the flesh and blood of my body dry up; I shall not give up my efforts so long as I have not attained whatever is attainable by manly perseverance, energy and endeavor.[90]

Nothing worthwhile, least of all true happiness, could be attained without tremendous effort and a total reorienting of our lives. The Buddha left no doubt on this point nor on the allure of the unreal world of passing existence to deflect us from our goal.

7. *Right Mindfulness:* The Buddha believed that evil lay in the mind, not in the will, that ignorance, not informed choice, is the source of all malice and suffering. The degree of mental control and insight demanded of the adept may well shock the Westerner, accustomed to so much

stimulation from the environment and to manipulation by the electronic media. The Buddha urges his followers to meditate on their bodies, minds, emotions and on the phenomena that float in and out of consciousness. They are called to visualize the most disgusting sights imaginable and learn to control all fear and emotional response.

Like the trainer who stakes the elephant to the ground and domesticates him by repeated discipline, so each searcher must learn to so concentrate that one achieves total and unwavering mental control of one's consciousness. There eventuates, after long practice, a person oblivious of external distractions and internal fantasies.[91] One is truly experiencing the penultimate stage of enlightenment and freedom from dependency on undependable diversions.

8. *Right Concentration:* This final stage is also—perhaps better— referred to as "right absorption." In this final level the individual passes beyond pain and pleasure, beyond joy and grief into the total and ineffable experience of Nirvana, the absorption in peace, discernment and enlightenment. The individual is a "new" creature according to the Buddha. In a sense one has "completed" one's being and not just become wiser. One has broken beyond all the limiting constructs of partial myths and experienced reality as it is.

If we find this incomprehensible it is very understandable. We should note, however, that there have been persons in all eras, from all cultures and within all religious and humanistic traditions who have echoed this very conclusion.[92] If the Buddha's teachings seem extraordinarily difficult to follow, it must be noted that he never asked anyone to believe but rather to experience, not to take his insights on faith, but to rely on their own powers of observation and to risk their own personal journey. It is no coincidence that statues of the Buddha invariably depict him with a blissful look. Buddhists are expressing their conviction that not only he, but all humankind, can experience their Buddha-nature by personally appropriating the Four Noble Truths as their dearest treasure. To avoid the journey towards enlightenment because of the arduousness of the task is inevitably to mire ourselves in a world of illusion and to condemn ourselves to an endless repetition of rebirths where suffering and pain will be confronted over and over again.

The reader whose religious concepts have been shaped within the Judeo-Christian tradition may well find a central question arising in consciousness: is there any place for God within Buddhism? The question is important but the answer is complex. The Buddha never denied God but he never affirmed God either. He considered the question of God's existence to be irrelevant for two reasons: 1. Since the law of *karma* is the law of the universe, if a God existed He would be bound by this same immutable law of cause and effect and could do nothing to alter it. Speculation on the existence of a God or gods removed one, as in Hinduism, the Buddha believed, from the task of assuming responsibility for one's own life. This conclusion would be stressed, many centuries later, by Karl Marx in his critique of religion and its "world disdain." 2. If there were a God, supposedly all-powerful and all-loving, how could He create a world of such suffering and imperfection? The Buddhist theodicy (the philosophy concerned with coalescing belief in God and the problem of evil) simply rejected any possibility of connecting the two. The question of a Supreme Being does not enter the mind of a traditional Buddhist.[93]

When the Moslems invaded India in the twelfth century A.D. they systematically destroyed Buddhist temples and massacred monks and nuns, so offended were they by these "atheists." And yet Buddhism, in its historical development, has manifested, in its more popular forms, theistic elements.

Originally Buddhism demanded a total commitment of the individual in a monastic environment and the convert was expected to devote his or her[94] life to full-time pursuit of his or her goal. The Buddhist cherished the "Three Jewels," the Buddha, the Dharma (teaching) and the Sangha (religious community). Lay persons who could not leave their families or occupations were related to the monasteries by supporting the monks and nuns, but these laypersons were not fully members of the monastic community.

Gradually the basic religious needs of the laity were unmet because the non-intellectual masses found little comfort in what was perceived as an overly rational system. As Buddhism spread outside India it began to absorb many local customs and superstitions that the Buddha had vehemently rejected. In many cases the original message of the Buddha became diluted as it encountered indigenous religious and animistic practices. By the end of the third century B.C. popular piety became increasingly remote from the monastic discipline and began to generate a cult of devotional theism in which the Buddha was held to be a living god receptive to prayer and devotion:[95]

> The religious longing and need of the average layman first expressed itself within the context of the new beliefs through the growing adoration and homage that was paid to the Buddha himself. It was supported by the ingrained habit of the laity to turn to these men and deities who were beyond the restrictions of earthly life either because of their initial nature as deities or their attained stature as beings who were now free. . . . Both the laity and many of the Sangha brought with them into Buddhism the religious traditions which were part of their cultural environment and an essential need to their understanding of existence.[96]

Buddhism evolved into two main schools, Hinayana ("Small Vehicle") and Mahayana ("Great Vehicle"). The former tends to be more conservative, more monastic, and adheres to the ideal of the (*arhat*) or wise man. Hinayanists generally regard as erroneous the schools of Mahayana (there are many subdivisions and thousands of sacred books) which tend to be more liberal, progressive and speculative.

The term "Hinayana" is seen as derogatory and these Buddhists refer to themselves as *Theravada*, "The Way of the Elders." Mahayanists see the former as too inflexible and they prefer the ideal of the *bodhisattva*, or compassionate one. A parallel between the two schools would be that existing between Roman Catholicism and Protestantism.[97]

Geographically, Theravada spread into Sri Lanka, Burma, Thailand and Cambodia. It is also known as the Southern School. Mahayana spread into Mongolia, China, Tibet, Korea and Japan and is also known as the Northern School. A third category of Buddhism is Tibetan, an offshoot of

Mahayana incorporating animism, magic, superstition and polytheism in ways peculiar to this region. It is sometimes called Tantric Buddhism.

Many Westerners are familiar with Zen Buddhism in popular writings of Alan Watts and other authors. Although it is a form of Mahayana it also incorporates elements of Chinese Taoism and appears to resemble Theravada Buddhism in its strict discipline. The goal of Zen is *satori* (enlightenment) and this Japanese Buddhism strictly enjoins its adherents to resist all temptation to rely on any external authorities. Zen monks will sometimes destroy Buddhist scriptures, deny that the Buddha ever existed and then burst out laughing. Their point is that all social and personal mental constructs are obstacles to attaining true enlightenment. The employment of a *koan*, a paradoxical statement seemingly nonsensical, aids the initiate under the direction of a *roshi* (guide) to break through the limitations of thought and to experience ultimate reality. An example of a koan is, "What is the sound of the color blue?" The values of Zen may appear to be questionable to the average Westerner but the Zen Buddhist believes our rational epistemologies are blinders, not avenues, to reality.[98]

Where Theravada has been the prevailing form, Buddhism has had the most impact on society because of the belief in Buddhism as not just a private journey but as a civilization, a way of life and a culture. Theravada Buddhism seeks a society where certain values are given political, economic, and social expression in the life of the people.

Mahayana Buddhism is more of a metaphysical system concerned with cultic practices and it lent itself more easily to accommodation with indigenous religions and thought patterns. Mahayana placed great emphasis on religious speculation about the Dharmakaya or the Absolute ground of all being. Concern about changing the social order has been less apparent, although Buddhism, in whatever form, has had a major impact on the value system of each country it entered.

Buddhism has played a major role in the context of Eastern cultures, and like the major theistic religions of the world, has placed strong emphasis upon future life. Because of its central themes, however, Buddhism has generally been more retiring from world affairs than most of the theistic religions. The present is important because it is when the potential for enlightenment is capable of being realized, but history does not have the same significance for the Buddhist East as it does for Jewish, Christian and Moslem peoples. The challenge of increasing technological change will present Buddhism with the opportunity for further refining its central beliefs in the future and of applying its spiritual insights to potentially dehumanizing trends common in so-called advanced societies.

Buddhism is a great cultural and social tradition that provides a method for changing consciousness, of changing one's sense of identity and of one's experience of being alive. Like all vital movements, Buddhism has changed and developed as it moved through history and encountered new circumstances:

> Whatever changes it has made during its historical evolution, its spirit and central ideas are those of its founder. The question whether or not it is genuine, entirely depends on our interpretation of the term "genuine." If we take it to mean the lifeless preservation of the original, we should say that Mahayanism is not the genuine teaching of the Buddha, and we may add that Mahayanists would be proud of the fact, because being a living religious force it would never condescend to be the corpse of a by-gone faith.[99]

Whatever differences exist within Buddhism, all Buddhists share certain viewpoints in common: 1. The Buddha, whether revered as a supreme teacher or a supreme deity, has elicited personal commitment from his followers and has served as a symbol of unity; and 2. Buddhism, like Christianity and Islam, encompasses all persons within its message of salvation without regard to social, economic, ethnic or geographical criteria.

The teachings and example of the compassionate Buddha have taken root in many ways. The long tradition of scholarship and learning in Buddhist nations, equality of opportunity bereft of frantic economic competition, respect for the environment, and a concomitant abhorrence of exploitation, colonialism, and extravagant consumption are visible fruits of the Buddhist myth and needed correctives to many of the myopic social and economic patterns of more affluent societies.

The wise Buddha stands today as a continuing symbol of the human quest for meaning and purpose within a world of traditional and often unsatisfying answers to our most pressing questions. The Buddha challenged current myths and assumptions about reality and turned the current wisdom upside-down. His persistent call for fidelity to our own experience and for courage in facing our most persistent misgivings about the current state of affairs echoes throughout the ages. When he died in his eightieth year, the Buddha's final words were ones of both negation and encouragement: "Decay is inherent in all component things. Work out your salvation with diligence." The Buddhist myth of the search for peace and enlightenment beyond all the transitory elements of life provides meaning for millions of human beings who are convinced that possession of happiness is found where one would least expect to find it.

Glossary

Animism is the belief that spirit beings inhabit the world.

Ephemeral means passing, lasting briefly.

Phenomenal refers to sense perception.

Study Questions

1. Which 20th century ideology used the word "Aryan" and what were the consequences?

2. What are the Four Sights? The Four Noble Truths?

3. Why is it inappropriate to liken Nirvana to heaven?

4. Why does a Hindu believe that the caste system is totally fair and logical?

5. Compare Hinduism with Buddhism and explain what they have in common and where they differ.

6. Do some research on Pure Land Buddhism and the role of Amida. Discuss the implications for Buddhist-Christian dialogue.

Further Reading

1. John B. Cobb, Jr., *Beyond Dialogue* (Philadelphia: Fortress Press, 1982).

2. Carrin Dunne, *Buddha and Jesus: Conversations* (Springfield, IL: Templegate, 1975).

3. Christmas Humphreys, *Exploring Buddhism* (Wheaton, IL: Quest, 1974).

4. Trevor Ling, *The Buddha* (New York: Pelican, 1976).

5. Charles S. Prebish, *American Buddhism* (North Scituate, MA: Duxbury, 1979).

6. D.T. Suzuki, *Outlines of Mahayana Buddhism* (New York: Schocken, 1963).

8.

The Christ:
The Myth of the Person

"If, as Christians believe, the martyr was at the same time the Messiah then his death has a cosmic importance."[100] These thoughts of a Jewish professor precisely narrow the focus of discussion about Jesus of Nazareth and his uniqueness as a religious figure. Christians believe that Jesus was more than a prophet like Moses or Muhammed, more than a wise man like Confucius or the Buddha, more than a philosopher like Socrates or Plotinus. The question Jesus put to his followers is the enduring crucial question asked of each Christian throughout the centuries: "Who do people say the Son of Man[101] is?" (Matthew 16:14).

The author of the fourth gospel[102] expresses clearly the faith of those who accepted Jesus as Emmanuel (God with us):

> In the beginning was the Word:
> the Word was with God
> and the Word was God.
> He was with God in the beginning.
> Through him all things came to be,
> not one thing had its being but through him.
> All that came to be had life in him
> and that life was the light of men,
> a light that shines in the dark,
> a light that darkness could not overpower. (John 1:1-5)

Jesus was responded to as the culmination of God's saving presence within his creation made real through the events of history and through the words of the prophets. The overwhelming love of God for human beings and his plan of salvation is communicated in the person of Jesus. He was the ultimate sacrament (the visible sign of God's invisible reality) making understandable in his words and deeds the mystery of the hidden yet present God. John's proclamation: Jesus is God present in our human existence.[103]

This audacious faith in Jesus the Lord could not have been possible, indeed is not even remotely comprehensible, without the sustaining faith of Judaism as the matrix of the Christ event. Jesus was a Jew as were his mother and first disciples, and Jesus made the declaration that he had not come to destroy the Law or the prophets but to complete them (Matthew 5:17:19). Jesus spoke of unfolding the spirit of the Law, of spiritual evolution not dissolution. Paul, one of the earliest Jewish converts and an indefatigable missionary, understood this when he said: "but as the chosen people, they are still loved by God, loved for the sake of their ancestors. God never takes back his gifts or revokes his choice" (Romans 11:28-29). The debt of Christians to their Jewish brothers and sisters cannot be over emphasized. It is to the Jewish myth that we must briefly turn if the Christian experience is to be properly understood, and, further, if the Islamic myth is to be comprehended adequately.

The only possible proof for God's existence, claimed the Prussian ruler, Frederick the Great (1712-86), was the existence of Jews. His point was well taken. The history of the Jewish people, had, with minor exceptions, been replete with religious persecution, brutal domination by foreign conquerors and relentless discrimination and segregation at the hands of pagans, Christians and Moslems. What sustained them and shaped their destiny was the unwavering belief in the presence of the Lord God Yahweh who called his people into being and chose them, from among all the nations, as his very own people.

There was, to be sure, corruption, formalism, schism and factionalism throughout Jewish history, but the people returned again and again, sometimes by fear or expediency, more often by response to prophetic exhortation, to the source of their existence: "For you are a people consecrated to Yahweh your God, it is you that Yahweh our God has chosen to be his very own people out of all the peoples on the earth" (Deuteronomy 7:6). God had called no other nation but Israel His chosen people.

The election of Israel begins with Abraham the Hebrew ("from the other side of the river"), a nomad who migrated from present-day Saudi Arabia into the land of Canaan, what is now Israel or Palestine, depending on your politics. The age of the Patriarchs, Abraham, Isaac, Jacob and Joseph is the subject of controversy, but about 1850 B.C.E.[104] Abraham received God's promise that he and his descendents would play a major role in the history of the human race (Genesis 12:1-3).

Further migrations of the clan of Isaac and Jacob, due likely to regional famine and drought, brought the ancestors of the Jews into Egypt. Welcomed at first, the migrants grew to a sizable minority, but political changes occurred that led to the Hebrews becoming little more than serfs of the Pharaoh. Menachim Begin's wry comment to Anwar Sadat in 1978, during the Israeli-Egyptian peace talks, to the effect that Egypt owed the Jews hundreds of years back wages has historical basis. The children of Abraham, Isaac and Jacob were pressed into hard labor creating the extant Egyptian monuments that still awe the modern day tourist.

Yahweh inspired Moses to be his agent in leading His people to freedom and in recreating a sense of nationhood among the enslaved Hebrews. The Exodus event, the passage from slavery in Egypt to freedom in the Promised Land, stands at the center of Jewish history and is the symbol of all subsequent Jewish striving. What God wrought through Moses in the thirteenth century B.C.E., he continues to effect, in mysterious ways, among the modern descendents of Abraham and Moses. The devout Jew has no doubt, in spite of a long heritage of misfortune, dispersal and genocide, that the God of his ancestors is present to all generations of Jews.

Yahweh revealed himself not only as Liberator but also as Lawgiver to his people. The centerpiece of the Mosaic covenant is the Ten Commandments. The Torah or Law is observed to the letter by the Orthodox Jew, more in spirit by the Conservative and Reform Jews, as an expression of gratitude and duty to Yahweh for choosing them among all peoples to be his own in a special way:

> We ought not to overlook that Judaism through its Torah confronted the world not merely with a religious revolution, but even more with a reversal of social values. Judaism entered into the world as a proclamation on behalf of all the poor, deprived, oppressed and needy people.[105]

Under the leadership of Joshua, the designated successor to Moses, the Israelites returned to the land of the ancestors and were led by "Judges" or clan leaders. The Judges were gradually replaced by a king who was to serve as a unifying ruler. The first king, Saul, was succeeded by David who made Jerusalem the capital of the Jewish nation. His son, Solomon, built the first temple in Jerusalem, but after his death the kingdom split into the ten northern tribes (Israel) and the two southern tribes (Judah).

Except for the relative security enjoyed during King David's reign, the Jewish nation experienced constant threats from more powerful neighbors. In 721 B.C.E. Assyria* destroyed Israel and in 586 B.C.E. Judah was captured by the Babylonians with the subsequent destruction of the Temple.

When the Jews were freed from captivity in Babylon* it was under the guidance of the prophets that they rededicated themselves to observing the covenant. This second Exodus led to a purification of Jewish worship and to the authoritative formulation of the Talmud or oral Law. Together the Torah and Talmud served as the pillars of Jewish practice and orthodoxy.

Throughout their long history the Jews suffered the burden of a succession of foreign conquerors, but the Law and the prophets sustained them in their dedication and gratitude to Yahweh. It was only in 1948 that the independent State of Israel was created, but the informed reader knows that it has not been a birth free of continuing pain or conflict. Jews, regardless of political positions on Zionism,[106] generally see the Land of Israel as intrinsic to the survival of the Jewish people, especially after the abject indifference manifested by world leaders towards the genocide of the Second World War. Jews pointedly note that it was not until a decree of the French

Assembly in 1791 that they were recognized, for the first time in Europe, as citizens with rights equal to others. This belated legal recognition did not, however, eliminate centuries of virulent anti-Semitism. History for the religious Jew has always been more than a chronicle of events and persons.

History is the locale of God's self-disclosure in human experience. The foundation for Western concerns for social justice can be traced to the prophets, those men and women who decried all abuses of power employed to advance the fortune or prestige of a few at the expense of the many. Whether religious or not, Jews are the products of a myth that has always insisted that God's holiness requires that every human effort be made to create social conditions that humanely and effectively address injustice and suffering. Sin is a human creation and can only be extirpated by the humble admission that individual salvation is impossible when the common good is ignored.

Jews believe they are the Chosen People, not because they are superior or more deserving than others, but because they were summoned by the Holy One to witness to his love for his creation. What appears to be a burden to the non-Jew is accepted by the Jew gladly as a reminder of the gratuitous bonding between Yahweh and Judaism. Life is a series of Passovers, an endless search for righteousness and justice, in the existence of the individual and the nation. God inspired Abraham, Moses and the prophets to risk their own futures and that of the nation to fidelity in him. This unyielding trust in God's continuing presence among his people and belief in his continuing revelation formed the basic strands woven into the life of Jesus the Jew.

In sharp contrast to the silence of the Buddha on God's existence, Jesus constantly focused the attention of his listeners on God as the source and goal of life itself. Human happiness, personal fulfillment and social harmony were desired by God for His creation and would be realized only if human personhood was seen as intentionally oriented to a gracious and loving Father. This conviction was, of course, the bedrock of Jewish faith through the centuries, but the followers of Jesus gradually came to realize that the relationship between God and his creation was radically changed because of the life and deeds of this man. Paul, one time persecutor of these very followers of Jesus, speaks clearly of the extraordinary transformation wrought in his own life when he became a believer:

> When anyone is joined to Christ, he is a new being; the old is gone, the new has come. All this is done by God, who through Christ changed us from enemies into his friends and gave us the task of making others his friends also. Our message is that God was making all mankind his friends through Christ. God did not keep an account of their sins, and he has given us the message which tells how he makes them his friends (2 Corinthians 5:17-20).

Because of Jesus, Paul confidently proclaims, creation and all of life are altered to such a degree that we need not hesitate to respond to God as a close friend, nor, indeed, will the follower of Jesus ever see things as before:

> Jesus was a practicing Jew from a conformist background, learned in his faith and with a deep respect for the Jewish tradition. Many of his ideas had Jewish origins. If he sometimes brushed aside the law, he sometimes—on marriage, for instance—interpreted it strictly. He showed a higher respect for the Temple than its own custodians, yet the core of his message could not be contained within a Jewish framework. He was, in effect, giving the Jews a completely new interpretation of God, and, in delivering his message, claiming not merely divine authority, but divine status. It was not a conflict on ethics. There were many ethical tendencies within the Jewish spectrum, and on this aspect accommodation could have been reached. But Jesus linked his new ethics, and the link was causal and compulsory, with a new description of the mechanism of salvation. He was telling the Jews that their theory of how God made the universe was wrong, and that he had a better. He was asking them to embark with him on a religious revolution. They had either to follow or repudiate him.[107]

Many Jews did repudiate Jesus, and his brief life seemed filled with conflict as he managed to array solid opposition from many factions to his message. Within three years—perhaps as few as one[108]—Jesus was executed by the Roman overlords occupying the Jewish nation.[109] The strange fascination of a person who wrote nothing, never traveled beyond an insignificant colony on the fringe of the Roman Empire, had no army or wealth, and was killed as a common criminal at an age when most men are launching their career leads us to ask: "Who was this man, Jesus?"[110] What did he do and say that aroused such lethal opposition and yet led others to confess him as Son of God?

Jesus has been portrayed in various ways throughout the ages: as Suffering Servant and as triumphant Lord; as Prince of Peace and as a contemporary guerrilla fighter; as Good Shepherd and as Superstar; and so on. If we truly wish to encounter Jesus and not merely to fashion a caricature to suit diverse, often competing, interests, we must turn to the Scriptures as the source for comprehending the basis for the extraordinary response to a person who initially appears rather ordinary. The Scriptures were written only after the followers of Jesus had come to grasp his life message as having overwhelming immediacy in their own lives. In other words, the Scriptures tell us of Jesus through the eyes of those who came to call him Lord. Here we find the Jesus remembered and celebrated by those who came to recognize and to proclaim Jesus as the Christ, God's most loving message to his creation.

Jesus spoke directly to his contemporaries in a literary form known as parables, stories that invited the hearer to share the experience of Jesus and to know God as he did:

> Jesus was not proclaiming that God was about to end this world, but seeing this as one view of world, he was announcing God as the One who shatters world, this one and any other before or after it. If Jesus forbade calculations of the signs of the end, it was not calculations, nor signs, but end he was attacking. God, in Kingdom, is the One who poses permanent and unceasing challenge to man's ultimate concern and thereby keeps world free from idolatry and opens its uncertainty.[111]

The parables were not simple tales with a moral, nor were they merely informational, in the sense of learning "something more" about the world. The parables of Jesus employed familiar images, concrete and immediate, to invite the hearer into an experience of a new reality that subtly shattered all of the parameters of a former reality which seemed comfortable. Jesus experienced—and invited his hearer to experience—God beyond any human manipulation or control, but at the same time, a God who was breathtakingly present in every aspect of daily life. Those who have eyes to see and ears to hear, that is, persons of good will, Jesus taught, will allow the parables to usher them into the quiet core of their being, where God is most immediately encountered.

Jesus challenged the comfortable assumption of so many religious persons that our relationship to God is somehow gauged, perhaps even guaranteed, by external criteria: ethical severity, doctrinal clarity, liturgical precision. Said Jesus: "not everyone who calls me 'Lord, Lord' will enter the kingdom of heaven, but only those who do what my Father in heaven wants them to do" (Matthew 6:21). It became unavoidably clear that Jesus was suggesting that oftentimes what good people "did" and what a good God "wanted" were actually opposed. Indeed, the really "good" person may, in God's view, be the very one who is shunned and demeaned by "respectable" folks.

Consider this: a few years ago a famous blues singer died in a filthy hotel room in New York, her malnourished body wasted by alcohol and heroin. She had been raised a Roman Catholic but gradually drifted away from her religious background and entered into a number of disastrous marriages and publicized affairs with a series of parasitical partners. After her money and fame had evaporated she found herself reduced to prostitution in order to afford the price of a bottle of cheap wine to drink alone in her rented room.

As she lay dying she summoned a Catholic priest and was reconciled with her God. Subsequently, she was buried in a Catholic cemetery after she had been commended to God's mercy during a heavily attended funeral liturgy. Almost immediately newspapers were receiving letters of outrage from "devout" Christians who were indignant at the "scandal" occasioned by the public burial rites afforded a notorious sinner. This curious conviction that salvation is "owed" only to the self-righteous who have paid their dues by a lifetime of keeping the rules was one of the cherished beliefs demolished by Jesus in the parable of the prodigal son.

The parable, recorded in Luke 15:11-32, is well known. That is not to say it needs no reflection, especially since we, like those who were present when Jesus spoke these parables, can tend to be selective listeners.[112]

The prodigal son, who asserts his claim to his inheritance and promptly goes off and wastes a fortune—money, by the way, that likely represented a lifetime of hard work and careful stewardship on his father's part—probably strikes a strange note of sympathy in us. Who of us has not done foolish things and especially when young, viewed our parents as restrictive, perhaps reactionary? The extent of the younger son's gullibility in seeking to buy friendship from the opportunistic crowd is awesome, but not all that rare. History has known many prodigal sons and daughters who have acted this irresponsibly, so the plot is not really far-fetched.

If we are practical persons who respect the need for long-range planning, especially if we are not wealthy, the young man may appear to be an object of pity or scorn. Still, it would be wonderful to have a father like the one in the parable. No hassle about this depleted wealth, no private guilt trip, no yelling and screaming, no snide remarks about being a complete fool. The prodigal son experienced total and unconditional love from a father who valued his well-being before anything else he possessed. If we ever tripped over the edge and acted in such an irresponsible way, how comforting to know the depths of such love, to finally comprehend that we can forgive ourselves because we are forgiven by the one we offended. Jesus tells us, simply and directly, that God is like the father in this parable. We can go home again, regardless of what awful and loathsome actions are in our past, and we can be welcomed with love and total forgiveness by God. God is like this father and his love is without limit. The younger son is potentially each one of us in our propensity to create a world with ourselves as its center.

And yet, what of the elder son: what of our other role? If we can iden-tify with the unspoken relief of the younger son, we must honestly admit that were we the older brother, we would be in a state of rage—and why not? Here he is dutiful, obedient, and dependable and yet what does it matter? His self-centered brother goes off, wastes a fortune, embarrasses his family, returns home looking a bum and smelling like the pigs he was tending, and yet his father treats him like royalty. It's as though the younger son were being rewarded for being a bad son and the older son were being punished for being a good son. No wonder there is resentment, anger and disdain. Where is the justice, the balance, just plain common sense? Why doesn't their father teach him a needed lesson and let him know that he will have to earn respect and will be closely monitored to see if he has "indeed" matured? Why doesn't God act the way we think is sen-sible? Why not indeed?

Jesus was communicating a number of messages in this parable. To read it only as a classic example of sibling rivalry or of paternal overindul-gence is to restrict its far-reaching and disturbing implications. This re-quires of us that we savor the parable and not approach it in a detached fashion as though the message has no personal import.

The younger son chose his fate in a sense, but, like each of us, he ac-tually knew less than he thought he did. In another sense, then, he was a victim of his own immaturity and impatience. Jesus seemed less con-cerned with the cause than the condition of the younger son's existence: Jesus was not a lawyer asking his listeners to adjudicate blame or respon-sibility but to imagine a real-life possibility.

The son was himself assuredly but he was also all the broken, despised and rootless persons in every age. How would this parable, adjusted for the 20th century, apply? Might the younger son stand for those throw-away women we sometimes encounter as they shuffle along with shopping bags crammed with junk or near junk, dishevelled and faintly dangerous? Might he be the seedy old man muttering to himself in a door-way who causes us to walk a little faster when we see him? He or she is any one of a whole series of persons we find offensive to our middle-class sensibilities and to our cherished concepts of beauty, value and worth. We reassure ourselves that it couldn't happen to us. Like the elder son we might psychologically refuse to call such persons "my brother (or sister)" and refer to them as "your son (or daughter)." They are thus recognized as human beings but not as kindred who elicit a deeper concern. The unattractive creatures have nothing in common with the sweet-smelling and smooth-talking beautiful people who know almost instinctively that the choice of the wrong soft drink, shampoo, or beauty cream can spell disaster in one's social life. If these unfortunates have to be acknowledged, better to do so statistically and rarely, perhaps through the annual Christmas fund sponsored by the metropolitan newspapers.[113] If these individuals ever had a chance they blew it and now they have to bear the consequences. If they have broken under the strains of an unhappy childhood, low self-esteem, mental illness or some other personal tragedy, that is a pity, but there are social agencies to deal with them. Or so we would like to think.

The older brother is the personification of the conventional wisdom of society, a wisdom based on propriety, status and success, a collection of values held out to us as both sensible and unattainable. We are taught early on the essential nature of success. Clothing without the proper label is unfashionably utilitarian. Education geared towards a lifetime of enrichment instead of the first job interview is hopelessly impractical. The chic diners at a fashionable restaurant may be tricked into thinking that instant coffee is actually brewed, but such failures are few. The truly astute consumer is tutored in the fine art of making choices that make the proper statement. Looking good rather than being good or doing good has become normative in the attainment of the American Dream.[114] In the time of Jesus, it was "known" that God's love did not rest on those who did not look the part.

In matters religious this same pragmatism is often detected or at least suspected. Recent polls have shown that only the people of India define themselves as more religious than the American people.[115] One might be tempted to expect little violence or prejudice in a society where 94 percent of the Americans polled say they believe in God and where a percentage higher than any other industrialized nation in the world are regular church-goers.[116]

Jesus was fully aware, given the long history of foreign subjugation imposed on his people, that a "successful" deity was expected to create a "successful" nation. A God of power and might was more attractive to the powerless than a God of compassion.[117] A fortunate and affluent people, moreover, might well be unconscious of the ways in which divine autonomy is presumed to be restricted by national goals. American presidents routinely invoke divine approbation for their decisions and they echo one chief executive who declared: "Our government makes no sense unless it is founded in a deeply-felt religious faith—and I don't care what it is."[118]

Except in certain artistic circles there is perceived to be something distinctly un-American about publicly-proclaimed atheism. If these observations seem to be a digression from the parable at hand, it may be that we resist, like the elder brother, any challenge to our God notions and we want neither for ourselves nor for our nation a God who is finally free to act in ways that are both mysterious and disconcerting. Jesus knew how subtle is the process of inverting Genesis 1:26 and of fashioning God in our own likeness. We read only the written word in Scripture but we may easily imagine how threatening to the complacent believer were these seemingly innocuous stories presented by Jesus.

If one may surmise that some Americans see religion as another designer label, it is evident that many others are not at all disposed to such compartmentalization in their lives.[119] At their most vocal they confidently apply Scripture texts to nearly all aspects of behavior, private and public. They experience no hesitation in identifying the misguided or unrepentant "other" as un-American, un-Christian, and unethical. The possibility of rational discussion about complex issues is terminated when any opinion that could remotely come under the rubric of "secular humanism" is expressed. How God acts and how he expects his agents to communicate his will is not a matter of conjecture but of certitude.

If the status-conscious Christian is the elder brother in his Sunday clothes, the dogmatic Christian is the elder brother in his Sunday pulpit when it is used to proclaim the "good guys" rather than the Good News. In our self-centeredness, Jesus says, we are the younger brother. In our self-righteousness we are the elder brother. This schizophrenic self is only made whole and healthy when we reflect in our relationship with others the love freely given by God in his relationship with us. The Our Father that Jesus taught his followers when they asked him how they should pray reflects the theme of his life: love of God and love of others are two sides of the same coin (Luke 6:27-37; John 15:1-18)[120] This expression of our most genuine human experience is both proof and promise of the "Kingdom of God."

Jesus invited his listeners by both word and deed to seek union with a loving Father by repentance and sorrow for whatever in their personal histories kept them trapped in a self-imposed prison (John 8:1-11). He was severely criticized for associating with prostitutes (Luke 7:36-50) and outcasts (Mark 2:13-17) but that was the whole point. The younger son in each of us would be welcomed unconditionally by the Father if we merely sought to be healed. The teaching, then as now, was scandalous to the elder brother in us that resents and resists "unearned" salvation for those we judge unworthy (Matthew 20:21-16). Rituals, traditions, and propriety, Jesus said (John 9:39-41) became perverted when they became obstacles to the mysterious and unanticipated presence of the living God.

In many ways and by nearly every measure, Jesus was a failure, an ineffective utopian and romantic:

> Yet Jesus even at the time was well aware of something else, namely, love's futility in the world of material values. He loved the unfortunate ones, yet he also understood that once they came to know love's futility, they too would be turning against him. When all is said and done, the hard fact remains that human beings are on the lookout for practical and tangible results. The sick after all were asking to be cured, the lame to be able to walk, and the blind for their eyes to be opened—they sought tangible results. Yet love is an act which in this visible world bears no

direct correlation with tangible benefits. The passion of Jesus begins right here. With a touch of sadness he demurred on one occasion: "Unless you see signs and wonders you will not believe." (John 4:48)[121]

The pathos of the life of Jesus, from a human perspective, is that those to whom he spoke, whom he healed, whom he loved were finally disillusioned. He was envisioned as one who would liberate them from all the darkness of mind, body and history and so he was engulfed in the tide of their urgent expectations:

> Jesus gradually became the object of all their dreams. Although different people had different dreams to fasten on him, to the vast majority he seemed to be in the mold of John the Baptist or Elijah or any of the prophets of old, the one man who could become their leader. In the dreams of the ultra-nationalists, he would be the one to eventually drive the Romans out of Palestine, the man who had it in him to restore their pride to the Jews. The Zealots eyed him as a possible leader to fire their armed resistance. Finally, there were the women and old folks and the sick, who looked upon him as a holy man displaying "deeds of power" and healing their infirmities.[122]

Jesus had indeed come to liberate, to heal and to give hope, but few understood the real nature of oppression and evil that enslaves the human heart or the very soul of nations. Like John the Baptist before him, Jesus seemed to be a voice crying in the wilderness (Matthew 3:3-4) and he came to accept the inevitability of a shameful and agonizing death as the means of transforming human consciousness and of giving hope to the hopeless. The life of the fledgling Christian community depicted in Acts 2:42-47 shows that the followers of Jesus finally comprehend the profoundest meaning of his parables and the eschatological foreshadowing of the Kingdom of God in their simple communal meals. Before they became enlightened and courageous, however, they knew great confusion and fear. The horror of Jesus' death destroyed all of their facile theodicies,[123] exposed their self-serving attachment to him and provided the awesome illumination of the racial disjuncture between bravado and faith. The cross symbolized the utter and complete destruction of a reality his followers thought they understood and hoped for. The paradox of the cross paralleled the paradox of the parables but now puzzlement was replaced by shock, disbelief and unmitigated despair.

We can only dimly and inadequately imagine the emotional state of the followers of Jesus as they viewed the broken body of their leader draining of life and carrying with it all of their pathetic dreams of power and status. The passion narratives in the four gospels eloquently sustain Paul's assertion: "As for us, we proclaim the crucified Christ, a message that is offensive to the Jews and nonsense to the Gentiles" (1 Corinthians 1:23). The shameful symbol of defeat and death was put forward as the centerpiece of faith in Jesus as his followers spread beyond Palestine into the atmosphere of religious syncretism sponsored by the Roman Empire.[124] It would seem a curious tactic for those competing in the arena of a bewildering number of religious options based on fertility rites, asceticism, reincarnation, uncritical polytheism or emperor worship, all of which found the apparent glorification of violence repugnant.[125]

If the gospels had concluded with the death of Jesus, however, we could never hope to understand the radical transformation that occurred in the lives of his followers. In a relatively brief time this frightened and confused group of dispirited disciples, who had fled into hiding in order to distance themselves from the brutal death they had likely watched from within the anonymous crowd, were filled with unshakable self-confidence and absolute certitude. The explanation was simply too mind-boggling to be dismissed as a bizarre hallucination or as an elaborate hoax. On both psychological and political grounds their claim was certain to elicit ridicule and opposition; mere human cleverness would surely have fashioned a less outrageous claim about the dead Master. The disciples believed that they had encountered the Crucified One *now living,* a fact attested to in the ancient formula expressed by Paul in 1 Corinthians 15:3-8.[126]

First the cross and then the resurrection. All of their moorings to any familiar psychic landscape were fast disappearing. The touching story of Thomas in John 20:24-29 rings so true to the modern reader precisely because it captures the normal reaction to such an affront to our intelligence and sophistication. We may reasonably infer that Thomas' colleagues had manifested previously the same incredulity and that they had desperately sought to explain their experience as some preposterous psychic episode. Thomas could not have been alone in his reaction and yet "the mystery unyieldingly bends its weight against our hearts."[127]

The myth of Jesus cannot be comprehended apart from the Easter event, and theologians agree that the resurrection served as the light casting brightness and intelligibility upon the life of the man Jesus. This is why Paul could make the Cross such an electrifying symbol in his preaching: the locus of death was now understood to be the sign of hope, precisely because the apparent end at Good Friday was a prelude to the new beginning of Easter Sunday. The death of Jesus destroyed all human fears of extinction and all bondage to sin. The person Jesus lived and died in the only world human beings know so that we could both experience and anticipate a transformed creation, that "Kingdom of God" he attested to in his words and deeds:

> The fact that the central representative symbol of the cross is always joined to the symbol of the resurrection is the final existential clue to the central meaning of Jesus' words, deeds, and destiny. For the resurrection as a representative symbol both recapitulates, reinforces, and intensifies the profound religious meaning of this representative figure, this Christ, this Jesus....He is the re-presentation, the Word, the Deed, the very Destiny of God himself. The god disclosed in the words, deeds, and destiny of Jesus the Christ is the only God there is—a loving, righteous Father who promises the power of this new righteousness, this new possibility of self-sacrificing love to those who will hear and abide by The Word spoken in the words, deeds, and destiny of Jesus the Christ.[128]

The seeming paradox of life following from death continued as the infant Christian community spread throughout the homeland of Jesus and then into the far reaches of the Roman Empire and beyond.[129]

This fellowship of believers was fired with the conviction of being the new people of God, the eschatological gathering of God—not a sacred remnant; but the firstborn of the gathering together of all Israel, and eventually all of humankind: an eschatological liberation movement for bringing together all people, bringing them together with unity. Universal *shalom.*[130]

Their numbers grew rapidly as the poor and disheartened embraced a vision of human dignity based not on power or wealth but upon the unconditional love of God manifested in the life, death and resurrection of Jesus (Romans 3:21-31).[131] Periodic persecutions of Christians during the so-called Age of Martyrs did little to hinder their phenomenal growth. By the fourth century Christianity had effectively challenged the numerous indigenous religions of the Empire and was proclaimed the established religion. A religion with a Jewish origin employing Greek philosophy and inheriting the Roman genius for organization evolved into what is generally called "Christendom."[132] This religious-cultural synthesis perdured, more or less successfully, until the Protestant Reformation of the 16th century.

The tiny seed of the early Christian community recorded in the Acts of the Apostles has grown into a global religion of over a billion persons. Roman Catholics, Orthodox Christians, Protestants and a growing number of local African communions trace their existence to the Jewish carpenter who died a violent death two millennia ago. Any attempt to present a comprehensive history of the Christian religion would be far beyond my ability, but it is salutory to realize that the prayer of Jesus "may they be one, so that the world will believe that you sent me" (John 17:21) remains a hope, not a reality, in our own day.

Coming full circle, it appears that the elder brother has not only a personal profile but an institutional one as well. It is for this reason that the various Christian communities have increasingly, if belatedly, come to own the arrogance and self-righteousness which are factored into their own historical experiences. The fostering of tolerance for diversity of interpretation and for non-defensive mutual self-understanding is the unavoidable challenge for all who claim fidelity to that Jesus who sought to remove all human barriers preventing men and women from experiencing themselves as sons and daughters of a loving Father.

Jesus has aptly been called "the Compassion of God" by a contemporary theologian.[133] The One called the Christ, by those who accepted his vision of the way life should be, was believed in precisely because he shared the human condition totally. If the Kingdom of God was to be attained perfectly in a future age, Jesus said, the foundation must be grounded in all of our imperfect and groping efforts to respond to the loving Father within this often unloving world of ours. Jesus gave his life for this conviction in order that the world would know that human suffering, ignorance, disappointment, fear and cruelty were capable of being transformed into a new creation of hope, forgiveness, justice, peace and love. Jesus was judged by many to be a fool, a charlatan or a deluded megalomaniac, but ironically Paul says, "God purposely chose what the world considered nonsense in order to shame the wise, and he chose what the world considers weak in order to shame the powerful." (1 Corinthians 1:27)

Lesser gods, be they power, wealth, status or some other form of glitter, would deflect us from our true heritage and destiny, if they were allowed to claim our first allegiance. The stunning paradox of Jesus was eloquent testimony to his teaching that the love of God is simply incapable of being ultimately vanquished by any system or condition of human fashioning nor of being replaced by anything less lovable than God himself. The divine spark within each person would flare into intense flame when the human heart gave up its illusions and responded to the Father with trust and confidence. In his teachings and his actions Jesus showed that in our grasping for certitude and security we often risk misunderstanding how graciously and unpredictably God reaches out to us. Unquestionably human wisdom would have elected Rome, not Jerusalem, as the location for the message of Jesus.

If God is present in surprise He is not absent in suffering, and this is perhaps the most profoundly satisfying lesson that the follower of Jesus learns when he or she enters into the unavoidable pain of human existing in this world of ours. Jesus accepted his death, not because he enjoyed pain, but because he found the Father's light in the very darkness that appeared to signal the end.[134] A new grasp of the paradox of finding life through losing it flowed from the death of Jesus and that death, accepted in obedience to the Father, was transformed for Christians into a manifestation of spiritual life and power. The Cross stands as a powerful sign of contradiction to all forms of legalism, superstition, complacency and oppression that serve to limit people from imagining the power of God and of themselves in shaping the present and the future. By word and deed Jesus called others to have faith and to show courage in removing from their own lives and from their societies whatever would enslave the human heart and prevent us from responding to God within our midst.

The myth of Christianity centers on that unique person, Jesus, whose life and death presented undreamed of possibilities for the human quest for meaning. Because of his complete immersion in our human existence, Jesus was seen to reveal how terribly serious God takes his creation and how complete is his love for all of us even as it often comes disguised in the histories of individuals and of nations. Jesus remains for the believer the most touching word of love that God has ever spoken to our world.

Glossary

Assyria was at its height of power in the eighth century B.C.E. It stretched from Mesopotamia to Egypt and had a long tradition of conquest, exploitation and brutality.

Babylon conquered Assyria and ruled the same area for approximately 100 years. Babylon was conquered by the Persians under Cyrus who then allowed the Jews enslaved by the Babylonians to return to their homeland.

Study Questions

1. How do you explain the paradox of anti-Semitism among the followers of a Jewish messiah?

2. Why was Jesus a threat to the Roman authorities and to traditional Jewish teaching?

3. Nietzsche, the German atheistic philosopher, once said, "The last Christian died on the cross." What judgment do you think he is making about Christians?

4. Read the first chapter in the Gospel of John and compare it with the first chapter in the Gospel of Matthew. Discuss the differences.

5. What are the similarities and differences between the Buddha and the Christ?

6. Read *A Life of Christ* by Shusaku Endo and discuss where the "maternal" side of Jesus is expressed.

Further Reading

1. Paul F. Knitter, *No Other Name?* (Maryknoll: Orbis, 1985).

2. Robert Masson, *The Charmed Circle* (Kansas City, MO: Sheed & Ward, 1987).

3. Albert Nolan, *Jesus Before Christianity* (Maryknoll: Orbis, 1988).

4. John Shea, *The Challenge of Jesus* (Garden City, NY: Image, 1977).

5. Gerald S. Sloyan, *Jesus in Focus* (Mystic, CT: Twenty-Third Publications, 1983).

6. Jon Sobrino, *Christology at the Crossroads*, trans. John Drury, (Maryknoll: Orbis, 1985).

9.

Muhammed:
The Myth of the Book

Islam, the faith of over three-quarters of a billion human beings, has often been perceived as a strange, fanatical and backward faith by Westerners. This is not a surprising development if one understands the long history of competition, conflict and conquest that has been shared by the Christian West and Muslim Mid-East.[135] The explosive admixture of Islamic nationalism and Western geopolitics has produced an intellectual fog nearly as dense as the smoke and chaos surrounding burning buildings in Iran, Lebanon and Kuwait. Suspicion, anger and ignorance distort the lens through which Muslims and non-Muslims, especially Westerners, perceive each other. Christians and Buddhists may view each other with curiosity, even courtesy, but Christians and Muslims tend too often to elicit mutual hostility, even disdain.

It is ironic that Muslims may remember too much history while Western Christians know too little.[136] Islam, like Judaism and Christianity, is an historical religion (*e.g.*, the central belief of reincarnation held within Hinduism and Buddhism discourages the idea of a purposive linear history) and has tended to interpret the amazingly rapid spread of early Islam in the century after Muhammed's death in 632 A.D. as divinely ordained. The unassailability of the truth of Islam was "proven" by the historical evidence of its scope and vitality.[137] Christian Europe went into a state of cultural decline and organizational turmoil—the so-called Dark Ages—at the very time that Islam was successfully creating a vibrant and dynamic civilization based upon the religious vision of an obscure Arabian prophet.

100

The resurgence of Europe, the spread of Sufi mysticism,[138] ethnic conflicts and internal corruption have been listed as key factors for explaining the decline of Islamic civilization. History now sadly confounds rather than comforts those Muslims who locate their faith in historical events, rather than in fidelity to the timeless message given by Allah to His Prophet and to all humankind.[139] The challenge to Islam is to revere history without being trapped in it.

Muslims ("those who submit") have a unique reading of the role of Muhammed and the emergence of Islam. They believe that Islam is not a religion and that Muhammed is not its founder. These assertions seem patently heretical until one understands that "religion" in a Western sense, as a set of beliefs or values distinct from one's "secular" pursuits, has no parallel in traditional Islam:

> It is a total and unified way of life, both religious and secular; it is a set of beliefs and a way of worship; it is a vast and integrated system of law; it is a culture and a civilization; it is an economic system and a way of doing business; it is a polity and a method of governance; it is a special sort of society and way of running a family; it prescribes for inheritance and divorce, dress and etiquette, food and personal hygiene. It is a spiritual and human totality, this-worldly and other-worldly.[140]

The "first" Muslim was not Muhammed but Abraham, the common ancestor of both Jew and Arab (Genesis 15, 16). It was Abraham ("Ibrahim" in Arabic) who first submitted to God (Allah), left his desert home in Arabia and traveled into a strange land under the impulse of an enigmatic but powerful communication from God.[141] Due to human perversity, however, succeeding generations either turned away from God or corrupted the message, thus leading God to send other prophets (including Moses and Jesus) to re-establish the proper divinely ordained relationship between God and His creation. In the Muslim tradition, therefore, Muhammed was chosen by God to receive and disseminate the final and complete revelation. He is known as the "Seal of the Prophets" because no further divine revelation is necessary or possible.

Over a period of some twenty years God communicated His divine will and a detailed list of social responsibilities incumbent on all human beings. Submission to these truths would lead one to salvation, whereas human obduracy would inevitably guarantee eternal punishment. It was the divinely appointed role of Muhammed, an Arab of the Quraysh clan of the city of Mecca, to convince his unbelieving contemporaries of both the truth and the invincibility of his message, or, more properly, of God's message.

About five years after the death of Justinian (565 A.D.), Emperor of Byzantium,* Muhammed was born in Mecca, the most important city in Arabia but an insignificant backwater far removed from the wealth and power of the great cities of the Byzantine and Persian empires. These two powers controlled most of the known world, had acquired power, prestige and enormous wealth, and had developed highly sophisticated civilizations. One Persian emperor wrote to the ruler of Byzantium that together their empires were "the two eyes to which divinity confided the task of illuminating the world."[142] Arabia, by contrast, was a mostly barren waste inhabited by nomadic peoples too insignificant to serve any other purpose but to be a conduit of goods between the Far East and these two empires. Periodic alliances were made with one or another tribe in Arabia as it suited the purposes of the two constantly warring major powers, but these Bedouins* were seen as no more than pawns in the shifting power struggles. Anyone living in this part of the globe when Muhammed was born would readily agree that it was likely in the natural order of things to have these two sprawling empires controlling the destiny of millions. Like it or not, their power was overwhelming, their influence awesome, their accomplishments unsurpassable. It was beyond the realm of possibility that a threat to these empires could come elsewhere but from each other. Common sense would reject any other scenario as outrageous. In this instance, as in so many other cases, common sense was to prove an unreliable guide to future events.

Very little is known for sure about the childhood of Muhammed, although pious legends helped to fill that void over the centuries. The birth date of Muhammed is generally taken as 570 or 571 A.D., but estimates vary three years either way.[143] It is possible that Muhammed was orphaned at a very early age, as all the traditions attest, and that he went to live with his grandfather. This arrangement lasted for only two years because of the elderly man's death. Muhammed is then said to have gone to live with his paternal uncle, Abut Talih, a prosperous merchant in Mecca. Much more than this is not known from the earliest sources, but numerous legends developed out of a deep devotion to the person of the Prophet.

The extensive proliferation of oral traditions concerning Muhammed was often based on political as well as pious grounds, however, and Islamic scholars have worked mightily to ascertain as much as possible the chain of chronology between the reputed *hadith** ("reports") and Muhammed.[144] The tremendous reverence for the Prophet throughout the Muslim world has led to a total rejection of all *hadith* criticism by many pious Muslims. The veneration of Muhammed by Muslims parallels that of Christians for Jesus and many fear that an historical treatment of the Koran and *hadith* is merely a veiled attack on their faith itself.[145]

The long history of antagonism between Christians and Muslims makes such a fear quite understandable and the reader should attempt to enter Islam through the heart of the Muslim. The devout believer in any religion seeks something far different from the detached observer from outside the religion. The *hadith*, then, give life and substance to this most extraordinary man, the Prophet of Islam.

There are many charming stories passed on by *hadith*. It is related that Muhammed had a cat he pampered, and one day when he was to leave his house he saw the cat had fallen asleep in his arms. Rather than awaken her, Muhammed cut off the sleeve of his garment and allowed her to remain comfortable. Such tales humanize the leader and teach important values in the process.

Likely Muhammed traveled with his merchant uncle and earned his livelihood in the way common to most Arabs until fairly recent times. Muhammed entered the service of a rich widow, Khadijah, when he was in his late teens, and gradually became her foreman overseeing her caravan trade. When he was 25 and she was 40, Muhammed became her husband. Muslim tradition has always held Khadijah in the highest esteem, and

Muhammed took no other wives during their 20-year marriage. He had a number of sons who died at an early age and four daughters. Of these, only Fatima had any descendants.

Athough the kinfolk of Muhammed were polytheists and Muhammed doubtless shared the common belief in gods, goddesses and desert spirits, something began to stir within Muhammed in his middle years. Like the Buddha and Jesus, Muhammed experienced a growing personal need to enter upon a journey different from that of his contemporaries. He was likely an introspective person who was sensitive to the social injustices of clan privilege, and who came to learn of Jewish and Christian teachings. How accurately these individuals communicated the orthodox beliefs of their respective religions we do not know, but they must have seemed far superior to the confusing pantheon of pre-Islamic Arabia:

> Arabs like Muhammed heard these stories and reflected upon them. Jews and Christians were sustained by worldwide empires and belonged to rich and powerful organizations. Their claims rested on sacred books sent from heaven in ancient times, revered for their antiquity, their worth proven by miracles. . . . The Arabs did not know these secrets, the Arabs were set apart from Allah. They must learn from those who knew, from the People of the Book, and so try to come closer to Allah.[146]

There were also individual Arabs who were known as *hanifs*, those who tended towards monotheism but could not embrace the Jewish or Christian religions because of complex reasons of ethnic and national pride. In any case, polytheism was not the only religious system current in Muhammed's Arabia, but certainly few persons in Mecca, Muhammed's birthplace, were monotheists.

Tradition tells us that Muhammed undertook ascetic practices, quite foreign to his countrymen, about his 40th year. He would withdraw into a cave on nearby Mt. Hira to quietly meditate, sustained in his solitude by the silence of the star-filled desert night.[147] What impelled Muhammed? What inner need had to be fulfilled? No records exist to tell us but we may surmise from what we know of the Prophet from the Koran and from the conditions of his birthland.

It must be recognized that there is a long history of shaping Muhammed's biography from polemical and hostile perspectives. Medieval Christians, for instance, learned in *The Vision of Piers Plowman* that Muhammed was a Roman Catholic cardinal who went to Syria after being denied selection as pope. There Muhammed sought power by tricking the gullible masses to believe he was divinely inspired. One finds further confirmation of this misunderstanding of Muhammed as a "Christian heretic" in Dante's classic *Divine Comedy*. He places Muhammed deep in the bowels of hell as a "sower of discord."[148] The first translation of the Koran into Latin appeared in 1143, over five hundred years after Muhammed's death. A translation appeared in French in 1647 and in English in 1649. Not only were Europeans generally ignorant about Muhammed, but the Koranic translations lost the power of the original Arabic:

> You will never understand this power and warmth of religion among us until you can feel in your own heart the poetry and music of the *Qur' an al-Sharif* ("the noble Scripture"). There was never music in the world before like that.[149]

Muhammed is mentioned by name only four times in the Koran. More commonly he is called "the apostle," an indication that Muhammed's personal existence is synonymous with his religious destiny. The role of Muhammed was to receive the final divine revelation, a revelation which is eternal because it is the uncreated Divine word itself. "We have sent you forth as a blessing to mankind" (Surah 21:107).[150]

According to Muslim tradition, as he was asleep or in a trance on Mt. Hira, the Angel Gabriel came to Muhammed and told him "recite." Muhammed asked what he was to recite and was told:

> Recite in the name of your Lord who created, created man from clots of blood. Recite. Your Lord is the Most Bountiful One, who by the pen taught man what he did not know. (Surah 96:1-2)

Tradition reveals that Muhammed was initially frightened by this experience, fearing he had been possessed by *jinn.*[151] He shared his concern with his wife, Khadijah, who assured him it was indeed from a divine, not a diabolical, source and he should continue to climb Mt. Hira for further "recitals." The revelations continued to come during frequent intervals for the next 22 years of Muhammed's life.

Although there is no chronological sequence in the Koran, scholars are quite aware that there were two phases of the revelation. During his early period in Mecca (610-22) 92 surahs were dictated to Muhammed, whereas his time in Medina* (622-30) accounted for 22 surahs. The Meccan revelations generally stressed the absolute unity of God, divine judgment and pain of hell fire for the obdurate. The Medinan revelations dealt with pragmatic concerns of government, the distribution of booty seized in battle and rules of conduct. During Muhammed's lifetime verses were written on palm leaves or any material readily at hand. After Muhammed's death these were collected into the authorized version during the rule of his successor, Othman (644-56). This remains the definitive word of God for Muslims.[152]

> Man emerges in the Qur'an as the great addressee of God and God as the supreme arbiter of man. Creation is the stage, and history is the drama with revelation as the "direction." The authority and the authorship are God's, and man is to do his allotted part.[153]

Muhammed shared this basic insight, meant for all nations, with his Arabian kinfolk: God's role is to instruct and command while ours is to learn and obey. Abraham, the first man to respond to Allah's call, had received the eternal revelation from heaven and had lived as a righteous believer. He had conveyed to his people the proper attitude of submission and fidelity to the one supreme Divinity. Other apostles, including Moses and Jesus, had also been sent to sinful human beings to confirm the original revelation, but human perversity and pride corrupted the divinely ordained relationship. Allah, in his mercy, chose Muhammed to convey, for the last time, what human beings must accept if they were to be saved:

> There is not one of you who shall not pass through the confines of
> Hell; such is the absolute decree of your Lord. We will deliver
> those who fear Us, but the wrongdoers shall be left to endure its
> torments on their knees. (Surah 19:70-22)

Muhammed's message was revolutionary for his time. The Koranic
revelations were to be accepted, not debated, and Allah decreed that He
alone was to be recognized and worshipped as the Supreme Lawgiver.
Polytheism was an abomination that was to be rejected by all God-fearing
persons. This teaching had important financial and political implications
since various clans in Mecca supported devotion to various deities and
received lucrative income from these practices.[154] Resistance, disdain and
persecution met Muhammed's efforts to preach this final revelation to all
his people. The economic and political underpinnings of an ancient clan
society would be destroyed were final authority to reside in an utterly
transcendent God whose commands were final and uncompromising.
"When Our clear revelations are recited to them the unbelievers say to the
faithful: 'Will that in any way add to your wealth or place you in better
company than ours?'" (Surah 19:73)

Many Meccans saw little attraction in the demanding message conveyed by Muhammed and so conversions to this new (or ancient) faith
were few for the small band of Muslims. Ridicule and persecution were
borne by Muhammed during the twelve years that he received revelations
in Mecca. Some of his persecuted followers fled to Ethiopia for sanctuary
but Muhammed remained in Mecca seeking to convert the *karifin* ("unbelievers"). The lack of success resulting from patient witness and from
preaching, however, led to a critical decision by Muhammed to enter on a
hijrah[155] to the city of Yathrib, known today as Medina, A change of locale and a change in tactics were seen to be essential if Islam were to be a
success and Allah vindicated in His trust in Muhammed.

Medina served to demonstrate Muhammed's administrative skills in a
city wracked by tribal, ethnic and religious differences. He was, by most
accounts, single-minded in his plans to create the *umma* ("community of
believers") of Islam; tolerance to the large Jewish community and to
pagans was extended, as long as neither group gave aid or support to his

enemies in Mecca.[156] This uneasy alliance did not hold for long, however, and military expeditions against any group seen to oppose the destiny of the *umma* to spread Allah's rule were routinely launched. Forcible expulsions, the seizure of property and the dispersal of tribes were judged to be necessary measures to consolidate authority and Islamic rule in Medina.

Jewish tribes in and around Medina were especially resistant to the Islamic hegemony preached by Muhammed and one Jewish tribe, the Qurayzah, suffered the massacre of 800 males and selling into slavery of their women and children. This occurred in 627 A.D. (5 A.H.) Two years late the Jews of Khaybar were also put to the sword.[157]

> Allah has promised you rich booty and has given you this (the spoils taken at Khaybar) with all promptness. He has protected you from your enemies, so that He may make your victory a sign to true believers and guide you along a straight path.

> And Allah knows of other spoils which you have not yet taken. Allah has power over all things. (Surah 48:20-21)

The primary opponents of the Muslims were not the Jewish clans nor the pagan tribes. It was clear to Muhammed that Mecca, the city of his birth, had to submit to Allah, and therefore the Quraysh, the rulers of Mecca, had to be vanquished. Over a period of some eight years the Muslims attacked caravans destined for Mecca and engaged the Quraysh in a number of battles. Each victory was seen as justifying the claim of Muhammed to speak in the name of Allah. In 630 A.D. (8 A.H.) Mecca was taken by Muhammed, the entire population converted and the Kaaba was established as the religious center of Islam. The invincible will of Allah was proven to be omnipotent in the face of overwhelming odds. A faith without power and worldly success was simply incomprehensible to Muhammed's world:

> The notion that God rewards the faithful is not peculiar to Muslims but arises in all religions where circumstances permit. Nineteenth century West Europeans, stunned by their military and cultural supremacy, often saw God's hand in their success, much as Muslims had earlier; some Jews, elated by the creation

of the modern state of Israel, drew cosmic conclusions from it. The difference is, this interpretation occurs only occasionally among Jews and Christians, disappearing with the first winds of adversity, while it characterizes and pervades Islamdom. Jews and Christians expect tribulation, Muslims expect triumph.[158]

Triumph followed triumph. Everywhere Islam was successful as Arabia was united under the Koranic vision and its impassioned soldiers now turned outward towards the Byzantine and Persian Empires. The spread of Islam was rapid and startling.[159] Within a hundred years of Muhammed's death Arab Muslims controlled a vast empire which stretched from Spain across northern Africa throughout the Near and Middle East through India and into parts of China. In the process of expansion, the Persian Empire was destroyed and the once sprawling Byzantine Empire was reduced to the city of Constantinople and the plains of Anatolia, part of modern Turkey. Muslim armies and navies harassed Europe for centuries, even to the point of attacking a monastery on the shores of Lake Geneva in Switzerland and of invading Rome and threatening the Pope. This vibrant faith and military success stood on a simple, if sturdy, foundation.

When Muhammed entered Mecca triumphant, now the leader of the once despised Muslim community, he was likely aware of the need to communicate the tenets of Islam in clear and concise terms to a people who had little patience with theological subtlety or philosophical abstractions. The appeal of Islam, on one level at least, lies in its ability to be easily summarized in the "Five Pillars."

1. The *Profession of Faith* (the *shahada*) proclaims "There is no god but Allah and Muhammed is His prophet." One becomes a Muslim by sincerely reciting this statement in the presence of two male Muslim witnesses. Contrary to later polemics, Islam absorbed great numbers of African and Asian Christians and Jews into its fold by offering an alternative to the often complex and competing Christian elaborations of doctrine or to the formalized and demanding legalisms of Judaism. Rarely was force employed to coerce non-Muslims to convert. Quite the contrary, since Muslims were exempt from the financial and social restriction im-

posed on the *dhimmis*.[160] Throughout the Koran the primary motivation for professing Allah and for accepting His revelation is fear, rather than love.[161] The profession of faith leads to acceptance of the other responsibilities of Islam.

2. *Ritual prayer* called for by the Koran (Surah 4:103) does not specify the number of hours, but in practice they are performed five times daily: at dawn, midday, afternoon, evening and before retiring. Prayer times, depending on sunrise and sunset, are often printed in newspapers, much as tidal information would be in American coastal states. The devout Muslim may say his prayers wherever he may be, alone or in a group, but he always faces Mecca and the Kaaba.[162]

The believer is called to prayer by a *muezzin* who chants in Arabic from the minaret, the tower flanking the mosque. The call to prayer is now commonly tape-recorded and amplified through speakers, much as Christian churches have replaced actual bell-ringing with tapes. Each part of the prayer ritual is marked by a change of position, *rakatin*, which are carefully prescribed. The Muslim prays with his entire body, a sign of Allah's total control over his destiny, and since purity of body as well as of soul is required, the hands are washed before praying.[163] The pervasive presence of Allah in His universe is acknowledged by the Muslim pattern of prayer throughout the waking/working hours.

3. The third pillar is the *zakat* or "alms tax" (Surah 31:4) which is an obligatory donation to charity. Islamic legal tradition has produced a complex system for assessing this tax, but generally it is accepted to be 2 1/2 percent of the amount of cash an individual has in savings or investments in a given year.[164]

Although modern Islamic nations have tax collections that are foreign to early Islam, each Muslim is called to respond to the needs of the unfortunate in recognition of the fact that all material goods are gifts of Allah who is their ultimate possessor.

4. The *fast of the month of Ramadan* is the fourth pillar of Islam. Ramadan is one of the twelve months of the lunar calendar employed by Muslims. Ramadan occurs on different dates of the Gregorian calendar

used in most of the world. The first day of the first year corresponds to July 15, 633 A.D.[165]

Ramadan is especially important to Muslims for two reasons: 1. Muhammed received his first revelations in this month; and 2. Muhammed and his first *umma* defeated the Meccan forces in the Battle of Badr in 624 A.D. (3 A.H)

Unless there is a condition of pregnancy, nursing, illness or transit, each adult Muslim is required to abstain from food, liquids, tobacco and sexual intercourse from sunrise to sunset during Ramadan.[166] Islam is not puritanical in matters of the flesh, unlike Christian teaching in various eras, but it does value the need for moderation and for spiritual "pauses" in one's daily activity.

5. The pilgrimage, *haji,* to Mecca is the last pillar of the faith and is required of all Muslims, male and female, at least once in one's lifetime.[167] Men and women wear simple white costumes during *haji* and no sign of rank or status is permitted. A janitor may camp in a tent, whereas a king may stay in a luxury hotel while on pilgrimage, but they are equal before Allah when they enter Mecca.[168] When the *haji* is completed the men have their heads shaved and the women have their hair cut. Such actions are presumably a sign of humility and also a badge of recognition. Once a *haji* (pilgrim) returns to his/her country he/she is accorded a special respect, secure in the knowledge that death will not find them unprepared.

The original purpose of the *haji* intended by Muhammed was to unify the people of the Arabian peninsula since the danger of clan civil war was always present. Today, when nearly two million pilgrims converge on Mecca in a given year, the *haji* serves to unite an international, polyglot, multi-racial body of believers. In eradicating, if even only temporarily, the class, racial and ethnic distinctions of the human race in the requirement of a universal white garb for all *haji,* Islam presents a model of tolerance and of our ultimate insignificance before the omnipotent Allah.

Muhammed is the most common male name in the world. That millions of devout Muslims name their sons after the Prophet of Islam speaks to the special veneration reserved for this seventh century religious figure.[169] When he was born, Muhammed entered a fractious Arabian world of clan loyalty, polytheism, female infanticide and petty ethnic squabbles. Byzantium and Persia controlled the known world and dominated everywhere with their culture, their religion and their armies. When he died, Muhammed had bequeathed to his Arab kinfolk a special sense of their uniqueness in Allah's plan for human destiny. The Koran was poetry and revelation such as the world had never known, and it was to an Arab prophet that Allah had communicated His final and unalterable message to His creatures. Loyalty to Allah replaced, gradually it is true, first duty to one's clan. The pantheon of pre-Islamic deities was banished to oblivion when the fierce monotheism of Allah appeared. Respect for widows, orphans and women in general[170] slowly superseded the barbaric patterns of a desert warrior society and all human activity was seen to fall under the final and frightening judgment of Allah.

Muhammed was one of those extraordinary charismatic figures who shifted the course of human history and shaped the loyalties of millions who seek to live out his convictions and experience. That Allah is in control of His universe is the bedrock of Islamic faith. That human happiness and purpose are guaranteed by unswerving adherence to Islam is beyond dispute. Muhammed is the blessed apostle who trusted Allah and, in so doing, provided the human race with all it will ever need for its completion and peace.

Glossary

Bedouins are desert Arabs.

Byzantium was the Eastern Roman Empire with its capital at Constantinople (now called Istanbul). At its height it controlled Northern Africa and much of Eastern Europe and the Middle East. Constantine, the first Roman emperor to convert to Christianity, had moved his capital here from Rome in 330 C.E. The site he built on was the ancient Greek city of Byzantium.

Hadith refers to the sayings attributed to Muhammed and passed on by oral tradition.

Medina, "The City of the Prophet," was originally the Jewish clan city of Yathrib, Medina is the burial site of Muhammed and is the second most sacred shrine in Islam. It is about 200 miles north of Mecca.

Study Questions

1. What are the Five Pillars of Islam?

2. Why do you think that Islam spread so rapidly and continues to grow today?

3. Who are the "People of the Book" mentioned in the Koran and why are they shown special respect?

4. Islam forbids any pictorial depiction of Allah or Muhammed. Why do you think this is so? Why does Christianity differ in this regard?

5. Research the period after the death of Muhammed and explain the division between Sunni and Shiite Muslims.

6. Visit a mosque and compare its interior with your own church or synagogue. What differences do you notice?

Further Reading

1. Kenneth Cragg, *Muhammed and the Christian* (Maryknoll: Orbis, 1984).

2. John L. Esposito, *Islam: The Straight Path* (New York: Oxford University Press, 1988).

3. Noel Q. King, *Christian and Muslim in Africa* (New York: Harper & Row, 1971).

4. V.S. Naipul, *Among the Believers: An Islamic Journey* (New York: Vintage Books, 1982).

5. Daniel Pipes, *In the Path of God* (New York: Basic Books, 1983).

6. Margaret Smith, *The Way of the Mystics* (New York: Oxford University Press, 1978).

10.

Concluding Remarks

During the last two centuries in the West, it has become a canon of our cultural wisdom that scientific reason and technological advancements would usher in an era of rational decision-making, peace and global material improvement. In this scenario, promulgated primarily by an intellectual elite in nearly every advanced society, the answers given by the various religious traditions would be found to be irrelevant and outdated.[171] Mystery would give way to empirical data, darkness to light, sin and guilt to psychoanalytical insights, and so on. The urgent questions of transcendent meaning and eschatological goals that all religions had wrestled with from the dawn of human history would be shunted aside for less grandiose and more pragmatic concerns: the eradication of disease, poverty and illiteracy; the building of roads, harbors and means of mass communication; the exploration of the seas and the skies. The list could be expanded indefinitely. The slogan of one megabusiness perhaps summed up the heady euphoria of two hundred years: "Here at GE, progress is our most important product." And another: "Better living through chemistry." Politicians adroitly coined their own slogans for public attention and image-making, even while appealing to those religious sentiments among the electorate that could be blended with our foreign policy and our economic programs.

Progress had indeed been made. There was no question that millions of persons on our planet lived longer, ate better, were housed more securely and worked under safer conditions, by and large. A chronology of inventions, discoveries and medical breakthroughs would detail an impressive list of human inventiveness, dedication, and courage. The historian whose profession it is to draw a larger map of human activity, however, would be bound to catalogue other, darker events that would be less admirable or even comprehensible.

The technology that freed us from the given limits of nature by marketing the telephone, the entertainment media, the airplane and the weather satellites in outer space was also employed to develop the wiretap, pornography on video cassette, the B-1 bomber and nuclear weapons. "Better living through chemistry" sounds terribly ironic as we continue to uncover chemical dumps illegally buried in our suburban communities. Which is to say that a price is always to be paid when human beings naively substitute means for ends and unreflectively accept the notion that knowledge equals wisdom. Science and technology, like all systems of human thought, are servants that have known many masters. The use to which we put our knowledge is never self-evident; our individual and communal convictions about the meaning and value of human existence are the essential touchstones for establishing a world that is more humane rather than one that is merely more modern.

When Jesus said, "Man cannot live on bread alone but needs every word that God speaks" (Matthew 4:4), he was undergoing an agonizing internal struggle in the wilderness. Would the seductive attraction of worldly possessions, power and status detour him from the journey he felt called to undertake? The Scriptures record that Jesus passed through this crucible of doubt and hesitation, but we should not imagine that it was an easy or swift victory. Nor was it for the Buddha or Muhammed. None of these major religious figures was running from life—the opposition and ridicule each one encountered demonstrated this courage—but rather each one entered a realm wherein the bits and pieces of immediate experience were seen to fit into a pattern of ultimate meaning that finally made sense of the dreams and aspirations all of us share. They believed that the quest they entered upon lay at the heart of the human struggle to be happy and at peace, and so they spoke and shared and endured.

The nuclear meltdown at Chernobyl in the Soviet Union has created a wave of anxiety in many parts of the world, forcing persons to ask if they have too uncritically paid obeisance to the high priests of technology.

Have we too easily deferred to the experts in the power blocs who tell us that the possibility of a global annihilation is not to be seriously considered because no one wants to start a war that no one can win? But for those of us for whom history is an unyielding teacher we are forced to remember that the two world wars in this century were never supposed to have happened either. Somehow genocides, holocausts, mass deportations and ethnic slaughters appeared with frightening regularity in our modern world. The lesser but more lethal gods of nationalism, racism, sectarian supremacy or regional hegemony sacrificed millions of victims to implementation of their self-righteous and perverted creeds. Had we forgotten those crucial questions asked by the Buddha, Jesus and Muhammed?: What is life for? How are we to treat our brothers and sisters? Are we owners or merely tenants on this planet? Is human pride or arrogance the supreme human folly? Is there a purpose to human existence that is a gift to be received and that finally is beyond all mortal manipulation? The answers to these questions will reveal to us what kind of myth we choose to live.

Those who tend to deify our science and technology in the hope that the unexpected, the tragic or mysterious dimensions of our fragile human existence can be predicted, anticipated or controlled underestimate just how limited all human systems are and will always be. The tragic loss of life following the Challenger spaceship explosion; the random violence that can strike the innocent who suffer from terrorist fury or domestic criminals; the loss of electricity or heat resulting from a winter storm; remind us that life will always entail risk, pain and disappointment. This conclusion is not a call to pessimism but rather a reminder that any myth that fails to speak to the deepest concerns of our being, that avoids having us face the questions of ultimate purpose and meaning, will not be adequate to the human journey of a lifetime.

The same judgment must be applied to those who confuse religious formalism with personal religious experience. A religious myth can isolate us from the very concerns that must be patiently and honestly addressed if we would be mature seekers after whatever light and truth we judge is available to us. Quoting scripture verses is not the same thing as reflecting on the experience underlying the words and actions of Jesus. Being knowledgeable about the philosophical implications of Buddhist tradition may well be irrelevant to the truth the Buddha taught to alleviate human suffering. Many devout Muslims may be able to memorize details of Muhammed's life without desiring to encounter the terror of a divine revelation. It may well be that the vast majority of human beings were never meant to be "religious virtuosi,"[172] but it is also unlikely that meaning or fulfillment will follow from living "second hand" the detached acceptance of the teachings of any religious tradition.

The point to be made here is that the Buddha, Jesus and Muhammed never desired to become icons or mere objects of devotion. (This happened to all three of these religious figures but only after their followers had undergone their own personal experience of reality each one advanced.) These men saw themselves as catalysts who sought to help men and women break through the deadening routine of their daily existence in order to see with new eyes and to live with new hearts a dream of a fuller and more complete existence.

The Buddha insisted that he was not the answer to suffering humankind's problems but rather one who invited others to risk going beyond the ephemeral seductions of material reality in order to find true and eternal bliss.

Jesus constantly spoke of the "Kingdom of God," a condition of peace and justice that depended on the courage and hope of average men and women to believe in a God who was always to be found at the heart of human existence. He asked repeatedly of those who sought him out: "Do you believe?"

The Koran tells us that Allah gave no assurance to Muhammed that divine revelations were to be assumed automatically (Surah 42:24). Muhammed was chosen by Allah to fulfill His will, but in no way was Allah dependent on Muhammed or on any human agent (Surah 3:142). Nor could faith be genuine unless it was a free response to the gift offered by Allah. Mere outward conformity was an insult to the true meaning of faith (Surah 22:11-14).

The Buddha, Jesus and Muhammed: three different persons whose quest for meaning gave the world three very different myths. The Buddha turned away from the material world to seek Nirvana and ineffable bliss. Jesus spoke constantly of a loving father completely involved in this very imperfect world. Muhammed spoke of a God whose will was supreme and who desired the absolute trust and obedience of all His creatures in order for them to be happy.

Which myth finally is "true?" For fundamentalists[173] of any tradition, the question is meaningless. Their myth and their truth is final and complete; all other myths, all other religious traditions are simply wrong and false. Two problems arise immediately from this assertion. 1. Most religious fundamentalists know little, if anything, about other religions, except as adversaries to be caricatured and debated. 2. Such arrogance—and this is really what it is—denies the authenticity and sincerity of the religious journey of those who wrestle with the questions of truth, meaning and purpose. Their self-righteous and parochial convictions assure them that God is incapable of being apprehended by any means other than those taught by their own tradition. Conviction often goes hand in hand with regrettable ignorance.[174]

There is no genuine faith—or atheism—without personal involvement and reflection. A myth that is merely a cultural artifact will prove incapable of satisfying our human hunger and need for both truth and meaning. I am a Christian, not because I know of no other myths or alternatives, but precisely and only because the person and teachings of Jesus speak to my own deepest experience of life and the mystery that grounds it. For this faith I am grateful. Such a conviction is never once-and-for-all, never a completed program, never a possession to be protected against a lifetime of change, growth, reversal, doubt and joy. Any person who grasps life as a gift, both mysterious and wondrous, will remain open to what Peter Berger calls "the dark drums of God."[175] He or she will be alert to the many subtle but significant signals that herald the dawn wherein God or the Absolute moves in our world. That experience will come to ground the myth that will serve to give light and focus to our life. When it is right we will know it and we will be at peace.

Study Questions

1. How do you explain the surge in fascination with astrology, crystals, the occult, *etc.* in our scientific age?

2. How has technology become both our servant and master?

3. What is the appeal of TV evangelists like Tammy and Jim Baker, Oral Roberts, Jimmy Swaggart, etc.?

4. Why do you think fundamentalist Churches are growing much faster than mainline Christian Churches?

5. Imagine the Buddha, Jesus and Muhammed having a discussion on the meaning of life. Create a dialogue that would show how they would agree and disagree.

6. On the basis of your reading and reflection describe the myth that best gives meaning to your own life.

Further Reading

1. Dom Aelred Graham, *The End of Religion* (New York: Harvest Books, 1971).

2. Thomas Oldworth, *Shaping a Healthy Religion, Especially for Catholics* (Chicago: Thomas More, 1985).

3. Dick Westley, *A Theology of Presence* (Mystic, CT: Twenty-Third Publications, 1988).

Notes*

Preface

1. Gordon Allport, *The Individual and His Religion* (New York: Macmillan, 1950), p. 29. Michael Novak, correctly, I think, faults Allport for his overly individualized interpretation—a Western Protestant bias—of the religious sentiment. See his *Ascent of the Mountain, Flight of the Dove* (New York, Harper & Row, 1971), p. 3. I simply wish here to note the great diversity existing within any given religious tradition even as the same ultimate questions are asked by all religions.

Chapter 1—Reality and Meaning

2. *Letters of Sigmund Freud,* selected and ed. by Ernest Jones, trans. by Tania and James Stern (New York: Basic Books, 1960), p. 436.

3. Albert Einstein, quoted by Lincoln Barnett, *The Universe and Dr. Einstein* (New York: Bantam Books, 1972), p. 109.

4. See Robert Ornstein, *The Psychology of Consciousness* (San Francisco: W.H. Freeman, 1972) for a clear treatment of this approach. A readable presentation of much of the current investigation into the functioning of the human brain is found in Gordon Rattray Taylor, *The Natural History of the Mind* (New York: E.P. Dutton, 1979).

5. Albert Einstein, quoted by Barnett, *op. cit.,* p. 108.

6. Freud admitted he never had a religious experience and then proceeded to reduce that of an inquirer to a psychoanalytic explanation that

*All references to the Old and New Testament are from *The Good News Bible*.

suited Freud. See his *Civilization and Its Discontents,* trans. James Strachey (London: Hogarth, 1961), pp. 64-66.

7. Joseph Chilton Pearce, *The Crack in the Cosmic Egg: Challenging Constructs of Mind and Reality* (New York: Pocket Books, 1973), p. 118.

8. I am here relying on the clear summary presented by Joseph Royce in his *The Encapsulated Man: An Interdisciplinary Essay on the Search for Meaning* (Princeton: Van Nostrand, 1964). "Encapsulation" is the condition of one who employs one epistemology as the exclusive approach to reality and ignores or rejects others. This might also be called "learned ignorance."

9. A "paradigm" refers to the basic pattern of perceiving, thinking, valuing and acting associated with a particular view of reality. It is a term preferred by scientists, although it has acquired a broader societal connotation. See Thomas Kuhn, *The Structure of Scientific Revolutions* (Chicago: University of Chicago Press, 1970) for insights into resistance to new concepts within the history of science.

10. See Peter Berger and Thomas Lackmann, *The Social Construction of Reality* (New York: Anchor Books, 1967), for a fuller treatment of this phrase.

11. Edward Sapir, *Culture, Language and Personality,* ed., David G. Mandlebaum (Los Angeles: University of California Press, 1962), p. 69. *The psychologist, Robert Ornstein, op. cit.,* says we relate to categories of reality, not to reality itself. He goes beyond a linguistic analysis and notes that we tend to see things the way that we have been conditioned to expect them to be.

The psychologist, Jerome Brunner, agrees with Sapir and sees language predisposing rather than molding the mind to certain modes of thought and to certain ways of arranging the shared reality of a linguistic community. See his *On Knowing: Essays for the Left Hand* (Cambridge: Harvard University Press, 1962), p. 137.

12. "Behind the tireless efforts of the investigator there lurks a stronger, more mysterious drive: it is existence and reality that one wishes to comprehend. But one shrinks from the use of such words, for one soon gets into difficulties when one has to explain what is really meant by *reality* and by *comprehended* in such a general statement." Albert Einstein, quoted in Paul Arthur Schilpp, ed., *Albert Einstein: Philosopher-Scientist* (New York: Harper & Row, 1959), p. 249.

Chapter 2—Religion and Science

13. Ernst Cassirer, *Language and Myth* (New York: Harper & Row, 1946), pp. 8-9.

14. Karl Jaspers in his masterful *The Origin and Goal of History* (New Haven: Yale University Press, 1953), speaks of pre-axial consciousness or group identity in terms of tribal myths and axial consciousness or individual identity based on reason. This is a process usually described as a transition from *mythos* to *logos,* from a world of ancient stories to one of self-conscious reflection. Specialists, including Mircea Eliade, Carl Jung, Joseph Campbell, Paul Ricoeur, Susanne Langer and Paul Tillich, have spent much of their careers expounding the techincal and specialized aspects of myth. For our purpose, myth will be used in a more general way to mean the various attempts to make sense of life, to give meaning to existence. This is the focus of such authors as John Haught, *Religion and Self-Acceptance* (New York: Paulist Press, 1976) and Edward Stevens, *The Religion Game American Style* (New York: Paulist Press, 1976).

15. Royce, *op. cit.,* p. 158.

16. The student is encouraged to investigate the viewpoints of scientists on this point. See, for example, the important work by the theologian and physicist, Ian Barbour, *Myths, Models, and Paradigms: A Comparative Study in Science and Religion* (New York: Harper & Row, 1976); also Fritjof Capra, *The Tao of Physics* (New York: Bantam Books, 1977) for an interesting correlation between Western physics and Oriental religions; and Werner Heisenberg, "Scientific Truth and Religious Truth," in *Cross Cur-*

rents, Winter, 1975, on the need to shift the focus from quantitative to qualitative approaches to life.

17. Mircea Eliade, *Patterns in Comparative Religion,* trans. by Rosemary Sheed (New York: Meridian Books, 1966), pp. 440- 46.

18. Paul Tillich, *Dynamics of Faith* (New York: Harper & Row, 1957), Chapter 3.

19. Sigmund Freud, *The Future of an Illusion,* trans. by W.D. Robson-Scott; ed. James Strachey (New York: Anchor Books, 1964).

20. Emile Durkheim, *The Elementary Forms of Religious Life* (New York: Free Press, 1965).

21. Albert von Szent-Gyorgi, *The Crazy Ape* (New York: Philosophical Library, 1970).

22. Allen Wheelis, *The End of the Modern Age* (New York: Harper Torchbooks, 1971), pp. 108-109. Wheelis also contends that scientists increasingly serve government and corporate interests before those of humankind.

23. Karl R. Popper, "Indeterminism in Quantum Physics and in Classical Physics," in *British Journal for Philosophical Science,* vol. 1, no. 3, 1950, p. 193.

24. That such a realignment of competing viewpoints may be evolving is the point of Martin E. Marty's "Science Versus Religion: An Old Squabble Simmers Down," in *Saturday Review,* Dec. 10, 1977.

Chapter 3—Atheism and Agnosticism

25. See Ludwig Von Bertalanffy, *Robots, Men and Minds: Psychology in the Modern World* (New York: George Braziller, 1967) for a scientist's critique of the "mechanomorphic" view of the human person fostered by much contemporary social science.

26. Novak, *op. cit.,* p. 97.

27. Herman Kohn and Anthony Wiener, "The Next Thirty-Three Years: A Framework for Speculation," in *Daedalus,* vol. 96, no. 3, Summer, 1967, pp. 705-732.

28. Andrew Greeley, *Unsecular Man* (New York: Delta, 1972), convincingly argues for the perdurance of basic religious concerns within all human societies, regardless of the apparent pervasiveness of secularization. See also the distinctions made by Joan Brothers, "On Secularization" in *Concilium,* vol. 81 (New York: Herder & Herder, 1973).

29. David Hume, "Of Miracles" in *An Enquiry Concerning Human Understanding,* ed. Charles W. Hendel (New York: Bobbs-Merrill, 1955), pp. 122-123. Hume believed that the "laws" of nature were fully known and understood in his era.

30. Jean-Paul Sartre, *The Words,* trans. by Bernard Frechtman (New York: Braziller, 1964), 252-253. Sartre is honest enough to add:

"I sometimes wonder whether I'm not playing winner loses and not trying hard to stamp out my one-time hopes so that everything will be restored to me a hundredfold." *Ibid,* p. 254.

31. Friederick Nietzsche, quoted in Ignace Lepp, *Atheism in Our Time* trans. by Bernard Murchland (New York: Macmillan, 1963), p. 138.

32. The awareness of being a *created* being is seen as the central religious feeling by the Christian author Rudolf Otto, *The Idea of the Holy,* trans. John W. Harvey (New York: Oxford University Press, 1971).

33. See Gregory Baum, *Religion and Alienation* (New York: Paulist Press, 1975), pp. 7-40. Also Louis Dupre, "Marx and Religion: An Impossible Marriage" in Martin E. Marty and Dean G. Peerman, eds., *New Theology* No. 6 (New York: Macmillan, 1969). For Marx's more extensive critique of religion see Saul K. Padover, ed., *The Essential Marx* (New York: Mentor, 1978), pp. 281-353.

34. The Jewish author, Elie Wiesel, believes it is patently absurd to talk any longer of trust in God after the Nazi genocide. See his *Legends of Our Time* (New York: Holt, Rinehart and Winston, 1968), p. 181: "Job never understood his own tragedy which, after all, was only that of an individual betrayed by God . . . ." Wiesel does not deny God's existence but considers that God may well be insane.

35. See the comments of Lepp, *op. cit.,* pp. 156-160 and Thomas Merton's "Apologies to Non-Believers" in his *Faith and Violence* (Notre Dame: University of Notre Dame Press, 1968), also Martin E. Marty, *Varieties of Unbelief* (New York: Anchor, 1966), pp. 65-213.

36. Contemporary behavior is strongly shaped by the common experience of alienation according to many observers. See Hendrick M. Ruitenbeek, *The New Group Therapies* (New York: Avon, 1970), p. 39 ff.

37. See Stevens, *op. cit.,* pp. 26-37, for a fuller development of these aspects of myth.

38. See Haught, *op. cit.,* pp. 147-173, for fine insights on religion and self-acceptance. Also the work of psychiatrist Karl Menninger, *What Ever Became of Sin?* (New York: Hawthorne, 1973).

39. See H.C. Rümke, *The Psychology of Unbelief,* trans. M.H.C. Willems (New York: Sheed & Ward, 1962), where atheism is seen as an interruption in development and as an indication of extreme individualism. Reversing Freud, Rümke argues that faith is important to mature socialization. Also Arthur J. Lelyyoeld, *Atheism is Dead: A Jewish Response to Radical Theology* (Cleveland: Meridian, 1970).

40. Michael Novak, "The Unawareness of God," in *The God Experience,* ed., Joseph P. Whelan (New York: Newman Press, 1971), p. 27.

Chapter 4—Experience

41. Carl Rogers, *On Becoming a Person* (Boston: Sentry, 1961), pp. 23-24.

42. See the preliminary observations on experience in John E. Smith, *Experience and God* (New York: Oxford University Press, 1968), pp. 3-20. His approach parallels that of Pearce, *op. cit.,* p. 150 who speaks of the relationship between perception and conceptualization. Also the role of awareness in constructing reality is treated by Claudio Naranjo and Robert Ornstein, *On the Psychology of Meditation* (New York: Viking, 1971), pp. 172-212.

43. Michael Polanyi, *Personal Knowledge: Toward a Post-Critical Philosophy* (New York: Harper Torchbooks, 1962), p. 3.

44. *Ibid,* pp. 300-303.

45. Smith, *op. cit.,* p. 64.

46. "Religious object" is employed here instead of the more familiar "God" of the Judeo-Christian and Moslem traditions to refer to that reality which calls forth our devotion, awe, or love. We shall see later in the book that not all religions personify this reality. For an extensive study of the attitudes elicited by the "numen" or religious object, see Rudolf Otto, *op. cit.*

47. This is a term employed by many humanistic psychologists to describe the development process of "owning" our experience and of relating to others in a non-defensive and accepting fashion. See Sidney M. Jourard, *Disclosing Man to Himself* (New York: Van Nostrand Reinhold, 1968) and the important essays in James F.T. Bugental, ed., *Challenges of Humanistic Psychology* (New York: McGraw-Hill, 1967).

48. Positivism, a philosophy based wholly on empiricism and the natural sciences, is usually associated with Auguste Comte (1798-1857), sometimes erroneously called the "father of sociology." Simply stated, Comte taught that human history moved through three stages: childhood (religion), youth (philosophy) and adulthood (science). This naive chronology presumes that only sense knowledge is trustworthy and that religion and metaphysics are outmoded. Classic examples of a positivistic approach to religion are John Dewey, *A Common Faith* (New Haven: Yale University Press, 1971), Julian Huxley, *Religion Without Revelation* (New York:

Mentor Books, 1957); and Bertrand Russell, *Why I Am Not a Christian* (New York: Simon and Schuster, 1967).

49. This compulsion to force experience into neat categories is common in many circles. See Peter Hartocollis, *Mysticism and Aggression: An Object Relations Point of View,* paper presented at the Mid-Winter Meeting of the American Psychoanalytic Association, New York, Dec. 17, 1971, wherein he reduces mysticism and pacifism to an attempt to sublimate one's aggression and as a reaction against the Oepidal father.

50. The reader is urged to consult the article by Fred Berthold, "The Meaning of Religious Experience," in *Journal of Religion,* vol. 32, no. 4, 1952. His distinctions among the phenomenological, psychological and ontological levels of interpretation are very useful in avoiding confusion on this point.

51. Peter Bertocci, "Psychological Interpretations of Religious Experience" in Merton Strommen, ed., *Research on Religious Development: A Comprehensive Handbook* (New York: Hawthorne Books, 1971), p. 38.

52. Paul Pruyser, *A Dynamic Psychology of Religion* (New York: Harper & Row, 1968) insists that we must study all the gods and ultimate concerns of persons in order to better understand the person.

53. Michael Novak, *Belief and Unbelief: A Philosophy of Self-Knowledge* (New York: Macmillan, 1965), p. 187.

54. "Neurosis" generally refers to a partial inability to function normally; "psychosis" refers to a total inability to deal with reality. It should be noted that neurotic behavior in one society is often deemed normal in others. Likewise, many geniuses and most great religious founders were judged to be "crazy" by some observers primarily because they shattered existing paradigms. For a critique by psychiatrists about the dangers of too easily labeling abnormal what is personally or socially disconcerting, see R.D. Laing, *The Divided Self* (Harmondsworth, England: Penguin, 1970) and Thomas Szasz, *Ideology and Insanity: Essays on the Psychiatric Dehumanization of Man* (New York: Anchor, 1970).

55. Devout Hindus venerate cows as the symbol of everything that is alive, as the mother of life. Moslems, Christians and lower-caste Hindus eat beef but the general population of India sees this practice as an abomination. The lack of a major market for beef in India has spared it the ubiquitous presence of McDonald's and its competitors, no small esthetic blessing.

Chapter 5—The Critical Analysis of Myths

56. The common treatment of conversion at the turn of the 20th century is expressed by James Leuba, *The Psychology of Religious Mysticism* (New York: Harcourt Brace, 1925), wherein faith is reduced to mass hysteria or nervous temperament. Religion was invariably seen as an expression of some other psychological disorder.

57. The traditional Reformation position of faith as a gratuitous gift of God, apart from any human striving, is best expressed by Karl Barth, *The Epistle to the Romans,* trans. Edwyn Hoskyns (New York: Oxford University Press, 1968). Barth makes a clear distinction between faith (a divine gift) and religion (a human construct).

58. Smith *op. cit.,* p. 117.

59. "Charisma" means a certain quality possessed by gifted individuals that attracts and holds the attention of others. Often a charismatic person conveys such personal magnetism that hearers will uncritically accept his message because it is *his* message. The possibility of dangerous and destructive choices is obviously a real one, since charisma is not the sole possession of altruists and saints. Adolf Hitler and Charles Manson evidently exuded charisma as do Pope John Paul and Ted Kennedy. Max Weber, *Theory of Social and Economic Organization* (New York: Free Press, 1968) holds that all religion begins with a charismatic individual.

60. The concept of "mature religion" is developed in Gordon Allport, *op. cit.* and remains a useful tool in the analysis of subjective attitudes within the religious experience. The classic work of William James, *The*

Varieties of Religious Experience (New York: Mentor, 1958), is still a major reference, after three-quarters of a century, because of his focus upon the behavioral results of religious convictions. The reflections of Aelred Graham, *The End of Religion* (New York: Harcourt, Brace, Jovanovich, 1971), are highly recommended as examples of authentic and experiential religion.

61. The study of the stages of moral development has been undertaken by Jean Piaget, *The Moral Judgment of the Child* (New York: Free Press, 1965), and by the American psychologist, Lawrence Kohlberg. A readable introduction to their work is found in Ronald Duska and Mariellen Whalen, *Moral Development: A Guide to Piaget and Kohlberg* (New York: Paulist, 1975). Kohlberg judges that no more than 5% of the adult population in any society acts on the basis of consistent universal principles.

62. See Mark Stern and Bert Marino, *Psychotheology* (New York: Newman, 1970), for the benefits to be derived from a Freudian analysis of religion applied to an immature religious development.

63. For an Indian critique of Christian missionaries see Vine Deloria, *Custer Died For Your Sins* (New York: Avon, 1969), pp. 105-128; for an African viewpoint see John Mbiti, *African Religions and Philosophy* (New York: Anchor, 1969), pp. 299-363. See also Thomas Merton, *Mystics and Zen Masters* (New York: Delta, 1967), pp. 81-91, for Asian examples.

64. This is the title of a book by Eric Hoffer (New York: Harper, 1965) which clearly shows that such authoritarianism is not limited to religious experience. Also Erich Fromm, *Escape From Freedom* (New York: Avon, 1967), links the need for absolute certainty to deep-seated insecurity.

65. Haught, *op. cit.,* p. 88.

66. The danger of creating hermetically sealed worlds of meaning is one faced by all disciplines. When R.A. McConnell, a biophysicist, became curious about the work of J.B. Rhine at Duke University, he spent four weeks interviewing Rhine's peers in the psychology department. One professor said he was familiar with the experimental literature of ESP and

that, in his opinion, if it were anything else but ESP, one-tenth of the published evidence would already have established the phenomenon. He further explained that personally he would not accept ESP because he found "a world without ESP a more comfortable place in which to live." See R.A. McConnell, "ESP and Credibility in Science," in *American Psychologist,* vol. 24, no. 11, 1969, p. 533. For another example of dogmatism disguised as detached empiricism see Raymond J. McCall, "Beyond Reason and Evidence: The Metapsychology of Professor B.F. Skinner," in *Journal of Clinical Psychology,* vol. 28, no. 2, April, 1972, pp. 125-139.

67. When we talk of a lack of defensiveness about exploring new areas of knowledge there is no implication that investigation has no limits. The sad spectacle of highly trained doctors participating in barbaric experiments under Nazi auspices is ample reason to insist that ethical and religious values must be brought to bear in many sensitive areas of study. There is a growing recognition at the frontiers of research that we may not do everything we can do.

68. A major study remains that of Gordon Allport, *The Nature of Prejudice* (New York: Anchor, 1958).

69. Walter Houston Clark, *The Psychology of Religion* (New York: Macmillan, 1958), distinguishes among primary, secondary and tertiary forms of religious experience. The former has a sense of vitality and immediacy about it expressed in moral behavior. The latter forms are more ritualized and conventional. What oftentimes passes for religion is actually social routine or peer pressure.

70. Joachim Wach, *Types of Religious Experience: Christian and Non-Christian* (Chicago: University of Chicago Press, 1951), p. 32.

71. Dionysus was the Greek god of wine and fertility whose worship was full of enthusiasm and emotion. All religions have had rituals, often spontaneous, that arose to meet a pervasive human need to be transported into a transcendent sphere. This has usually been balanced by the Appollonian or rational approach to religious matters. See Sam Keen, *Apology for Wonder* (New York: Harper & Row, 1969).

72. Sociologists talk of "plausibility structures" to explain the ways in which any society develops a consensus about what is "real" or "truth." The classic work in this area is Karl Mannheim's, *Ideology and Utopia: An Introduction to the Sociology of Knowledge,* trans. Louis Wirth and Edward Shile (New York: Harcourt Brace, 1959). It illuminates the process wherein experience is shaped and delineated and the factors present when a "new" view of reality is developed.

73. John Dunne, *The Way of All the Earth: Experiments in Truth and Religion* (New York: Macmillan, 1972), IX. In the same vein see Michael Novak, *Ascent of the Mountain, Flight of Dove, op. cit.,* and John Shea, *Stories of God: An Unauthorized Biography* (Chicago: Thomas More, 1978).

74. Freud rightly pointed out the price exacted in terms of conformity and deferred gratification by this process. It is the perennial conflict between individual rights and the common good. See his *Civilization and Its Discontents, op. cit.*

75. Aelred Graham, *op. cit.,* nicely describes this process as one of "enlightened openness." His own comments give this phrase its vital meaning.

Chapter 6—Three Universal Religious Myths

76. The beginning student may understandably be overwhelmed by the amount of material published in the field of religious studies. It would take even the most disciplined scholar several lifetimes to read the works relating to Christianity alone, just in the English language. The most sensible approach is to get an overview of the major religious myths and then to allow one's interest to lead into more specialized and detailed studies. The following works are by no means the only ones available but they are all readable and present a clear introduction to the world's religions. Most offer an extended bibliography for the student who has the time and interest to delve more deeply. Carl Herman Voss, *Living Religions of the World* (Cleveland: Collins and World Publishing, 1977); Lewis Hopfe, *Religions of the World* (Encino, CA: Glencoe, 1979); Huston Smith, *The Religions*

of Man (New York: Perennial Library, 1965). Edward Rice, *The Five Great Religions* (New York: Bantam, 1977); Hans Joachim Schoeps, *The Religions of Mankind* (New York: Anchor, 1968); John Hardon, *Religions of the World*, 2 vol., (New York: Image, 1968); Philip Ashby, *History and Future of Religious Thought* (Englewood, NJ: Prentice Hall, 1963); Allie M. Frazier, ed., *Chinese and Japanese Religions* (Philadelphia: Westminster, 1969); Lewis Spence, *Myths and Legends of the North American Indians* (Blauvelt, NY: Multimedia, 1975); Ruth Underhill, *Red Man's Religion* (Chicago: University of Chicago Press, 1972); Morris Kertzer, *What is a Jew?* (New York: Macmillan, 1969); Ainslie Embree, ed., *The Hindu Tradition*, (New York: Modern Library, 1966); John Mbiti, *African Religion and Philosophy* (New York: Anchor Books, 1970). Sir Norman Anderson, ed., *The World's Religions*, (Grand Rapids, MI: Eerdmans, 1976); Ninian Smart, *The Religious Experience of Mankind* (New York: Charles Scribner's, 1969).

Chapter 7—The Buddha

77. Ainslie Embree, *op. cit.*, pp. 3-8.

78. For a concise summation of yogic approaches see Huston Smith, *op. cit.*, pp. 32-61.

79. Rice, *op. cit.*, pp. 16-19. The system eventually multiplied to over three thousand castes, and, although it was banned in 1950 by an act of legislature, it perdures still, especially in rural India. As you might reason, the earliest converts to Buddhism, Christianity and Islam were from the Untouchables. In rebuttal, a Hindu will point out that the caste system exactly prescribes various obligations and places light burdens on the lower castes. Each person knows what is required of one and, if faithful, knows one will be reborn into a higher caste where one's efforts will also be clearly directed.

80. Embree, *op. cit.*, pp. 50-51; 62-65; 93-96.

81. See Graham, *op. cit.,* for excellent discussions between this Benedictine monk and Hindu theologians. Also the essay on Hinduism by Bruce J. Nicholls in Anderson, ed., *op. cit.,* pp. 136-169.

82. The reader should not be surprised by the legendary materials that surround the Buddha and all religious figures. Rather than being read as mere fable, the growth of such elaboration testifies to the lasting impact of the message of the religious figure and should be seen as a gesture of respect not as an attempt at fabricating falsehood. For a brief introduction to the Buddha's life, see Trevor Ling, *The Buddha* (New York: Scribner's Sons, 1973), pp. 87-147 and Peter Pardue, *Buddhism* (New York: Macmillan, 1971), pp. 1-52. Herman Hesse's *Siddhartha,* trans. Gilda Rosner (New York: Bantam, 1972), is a psychological novel that should not be read as history, but it is an accurate reflection of the Buddhist perspective. It has served to introduce Buddhist values into the West on a popular and understandable level.

83. Ling, *op. cit.,* pp. 66-67, for a more detailed understanding of the role of the brahmanistic priesthood in the Buddha's time.

84. A fairly technical but clear exposition of the subtle nuances in the Buddhist understanding of the Law of Dependent Origination (*karma*) is found in Ashby, *op. cit.,* pp. 101-116. Far from being deterministic, the law of *karma* posits total individual responsibility and freedom to pursue future choices different from past patterns of activity.

85. Ashby, *op. cit.,* p. 108.

86. Christmas Humphreys, *Exploring Buddhism* (Wheaton, IL: Quest 1974), pp. 52-53. Also Schoeps, *op. cit.,* pp. 177-178. An attempt to clear away non-Buddhist interpretations of Nirvana is found in D.T. Suzuki, *Outline of Mahayana Buddhism* (New York: Schocken, 1963), pp. 49-56.

87. "The Word of the Buddha" in Dwight Goddard, ed., *A Buddhist Bible* (Boston: Beacon, 1970), p. 32. Helpful comments are found in David Bentley-Taylor and Clark Offner, "Buddhism," in Anderson, ed., *op. cit.,* pp. 176- 177.

88. These Buddhist ideals have had curious consequences. Many of the early monks derided the common people for their mundane concerns and ambitions. On the other hand, Buddhism encouraged nonviolence, ecological awareness, frugality and generosity. See Edward Conze, "Buddhism and Asian Society," in *The International Buddhist Forum Quarterly,* vol. 1, no. 11, Autumn, 1978-79, pp. 47-54.

89. Quoted in James B. Pratt, *The Pilgrimage of Buddhism and a Buddhist Pilgrimage* (New York: Macmillan, 1928), p. 40.

90. "The Word of the Buddha" in Goddard, *op. cit.,* p. 47.

91. Very precise instructions on breathing exercises are an important element in all forms of Buddhist discipline. As applied in a therapeutic and easily manageable fashion for contemporary Westerners, see Herbert Benson, *The Relaxation Response* (New York: Avon, 1976) and Lawrence Le Shan, *How to Meditate* (New York: Bantam, 1975). Both authors will aid the reader in seeing the personal benefits of disciplined meditation.

92. Perhaps the best study of mysticism and one well worth the student's effort is Evelyn Underhill, *Mysticism: A Study in the Nature and Development of Man's Spiritual Consciousness* (New York: Dutton, 1961). Many psychologists have gone beyond the demeaning reductionism in vogue for years and now treat mysticism more positively. See Kenneth Wopnick, "Mysticism and Schizophrenia," in *Journal of Transpersonal Psychology,* vol. 1, no. 2, 1969, p. 93. Rice, *op. cit.,* pp. 84-85; Ling, *op. cit.,* pp. 16-18 and 120-121. The Buddha never presented himself as a deity and insisted enlightenment was attained by human effort and not by any super-revelation or super-human agency. The Buddha saw himself as a model of wisdom not as an agent of divine salvation.

93. Rice, *op. cit.,* pp. 84-85, Ling, *op. cit.,* pp. 16-18 and 120-121. The Buddha never presented himself as a deity and insisted enlightenment was attained by human effort and not by any super-revelation or superhuman agency. The Buddha saw himself as a model of wisdom, not as a divine agent.

94. Even though the Buddha held that women were fully capable of spiritual enlightenment, he hesitated to establish female communities. He

finally assented but added that this innovation would lead to a diminution of vitality in following the Dharma (teachings). This fear reflected a traditional patriarchal society and an awareness of the potential for disruption in human sexuality.

95. Pardue, *op. cit.,* pp. 21-28.

96. Ashby, *op. cit.,* pp. 95-96.

97. For a clear explanation of this historical development, see D.T. Suzuki, *op. cit.* He explains that Mahayana Buddhism is a logical development of the Buddha's teachings and argues the vitality of Buddhism in adjusting to changing historical circumstances.

98. Zen is generally regarded as medieval and irrelevant by most Japanese Buddhists but it has gained a following in the West, much to the amazement of the Japanese, for reasons too complex to analyze here. Suffice it to say that the purported secularism of our society may mask the unmet spiritual needs of many intelligent persons. For an introduction to Zen Buddhism see Eugen Herrigel, *Zen,* trans. R.F.C. Hull (New York: McGraw-Hill, 1964); Janwillem van de Wetening, *The Empty Mirror* (Boston: Houghton Mifflin, 1975); D.T. Suzuki, *Manual of Zen Buddhism* (New York Grove, 1960); and Conrad Hyers, *Zen and the Cosmic Spirit* (Philadelphia: Westminster, 1973).

99. D.T. Suzuki, *Outlines of Mahayana Buddhism,* p. 14.

Chapter 8—The Christ

100. Joseph Flusser, quoted in H.D. Leuner, "Judaism," in Anderson, ed., *op. cit.,* p. 89. The word "Messiah" refers to the anointed one who has been sent by God to His people to establish a reign of justice and peace. The Jewish concept of the Messiah was that of a human being, a major divergence from traditional Christian belief. See Joseph DeVault, " 'The End of Days'—Messianic Expectation in Judaism," in Sister Rosalie Ryan, ed., *Contemporary New Testament Studies* (Collegeville, MN: Liturgical Press, 1965).

101. The title "Son of Man" had definite Messianic overtones for the Jewish people. Cf. Ezekiel 2:1-21; Daniel 7:13-14; and Isaiah 53 for the dimension of suffering servant. The reader is reminded that Jewish expectations of the Messiah were very different from the subsequent belief statements of Christians. It is meaningless to go back into Jewish scriptures to "prove" the divinity of Jesus. *Cf.* Frans Jozef van Beeck, *Christ Proclaimed: Christology as Rhetoric* (New York: Paulist, 1979), pp. 112-14. It is questionable whether Jesus ever referred to himself by this title; but its application to him indicates the growing awareness of his uniqueness within the early Christian community. Also James P. Mackey, *Jesus the Man and the Myth* (New York: Paulist, 1979), p. 64 ff.

102. Gospel means "good news" and they are attributed to the four evangelists ("bearers of the good news"), Matthew, Mark, Luke and John. That Christian faith is acceptance of the living Christ and not only belief in the scriptures is clear from John 21:25.

103. Hindus who practice *bhakti* yoga believe in "*avatars*" or the presence of the god Vishnu in human form. The Lord Krishna is the most revered *avatar*. Hindus believe there have been a number of *avatars* (perhaps the Buddha, Socrates, Moses, the Christ) who have appeared in times of great human turmoil. The Christian belief in the Incarnation (the person Jesus the Christ who is fully divine and fully human) generally holds to a unique and final revelation with universal and eternal import.

104. Because they do not accept Jesus as the Messiah, but being cognizant of a nearly universal dating scheme, Jews employ the more neutral B.C.E. ("Before the Common Era") rather than the religiously explicit B.C. ("Before Christ").

105. Leuner, *op. cit.,* p. 51.

106. A properly nuanced understanding of Zionism would require a course in political science. Zionism has religious and political ramifications, justification for the creation of Isreal either being based on God's gift of the Promised Land to the Jews or on the reasoned necessity of a protected homeland. See Kertzer, *op. cit.,* pp. 153-158. When the Arabs say they are anti-Zionist, not anti-Jewish, they mean they are not opposed

to the Jewish religion but to Israeli political positions. Needless to say, the Palestinians read history, religious and political, in a way diametrically opposed to the traditional Jewish interpretation.

107. Paul Johnson, *A History of Christianity* (New York: Atheneum, 1979), p. 31. The Gospel of John 1:1-18 states the Christian understanding of creation and proclaims the divinity of Jesus. The rest of this chapter reveals the distinctive Christian belief in the triune nature of the one God.

108. The Gospel of John mentions three Passovers, suggesting Jesus was active in public for three years, whereas Matthew, Mark and Luke mention only one feast. Jesus, by these documentary accounts, was executed when he was between 30 and 33 years of age. This uncertainty should not lead the reader to doubt the ability of scholars to validly present the historical Jesus to our age. See Hans Kung, *On Being a Christian,* trans. Edward Quinn (New York: Doubleday, 1976), pp. 119-175 and Mackey, *op. cit.,* pp. 10-85 for a basic overview of the established facts about Jesus. The reader's attention is also directed to the careful presentation found in Edward Schillebeeckx, trans. Hubert Hoskins, *Jesus: An Experiment in Christology* (New York: Seabury Press, 1979), pp. 43-102. The historical reality of the life of Jesus is essential to understanding the Jesus of faith.

109. Jesus was executed in a manner reserved for the enemies of society, indicating that Jesus was seen as a threat to both the political and religious systems of his time. See Johnson, *op. cit.,* pp. 28-32. For a detailed account of his death, see Gerard Sloyan, *Jesus on Trial* (Philadelphia: Fortress Press, 1973).

110. Studies in Christology are numerous and of varying degrees of difficulty. Every reader will find accessible and informative John Shea, *The Challenge of Jesus* (New York: Image Books, 1977) and the excellent, but much longer, Hans Kung, *op. cit.* The advanced student with time and patience will benefit from Walter Kasper, *Jesus the Christ,* trans. V. Green (New York: Paulist, 1977), Edward Schillebeeckx, *op. cit.,* and Karl Rahner, *Foundations of Christian Faith,* trans. William V. Dych (New York: Seabury, 1978). Difficult but important is Frans Josef van Beeck, *Christ Proclaimed: Christology as Rhetoric* (New York: Paulist, 1979).

111. John Dominic Crossan, *In Parables: The Challenge of the Historical Jesus* (New York: Harper & Row, 1973), p. 27. For a more detailed understanding of the nature of parables, see Mackey, *op. cit.,* pp. 121-142, and Sallie Te Selle, *Speaking in Parables* (Philadelphia: Fortress Press, 1975) for insights into the role of parables in contemporary theology. It is accurate to say that Jesus himself was a parable of the Father. See, for example, John S. Dunne, *The Way of All the Earth* (Notre Dame: University of Notre Dame Press, 1978), pp. 84-93.

112. See Joachim Jeremias, *Rediscovering the Parables* (New York: Charles Scribner's Sons, 1966), pp. 97-116. Here he clearly and succinctly examines this parable and its close relationship to the kindred parables of the Lost Sheep (Mark 15:4-7; Matthew 18:12-14) and of the Lost Coin (Luke 15:8-10).

113. A radically different contemporary alternative surfaces in the life of Mother Theresa of Calcutta. This frail nun claims the parables call her to love Jesus in those who appear most unlovable. See Malcolm Muggeridge, *Something Beautiful for God* (New York: Image Books, 1977).

114. This assertion is developed in Waldo Beach, *Christian Community and American Society* (Philadelphia: Westminster Press, 1969).

115. *New York Times,* Sept. 12, 1976, p. 25. At the time of the American Revolution it is estimated that about 5 percent of the colonists were religiously affiliated. This figure had risen only to 20 percent by the time of the Civil War.

116. *Religion in America 1979-80,* The Princeton Religion Research Center. See also the detailed analysis of Rodney Stark and Charles Y. Glock, *American Piety: The Nature of Religious Commitment* (Berkeley: University of California Press, 1970). The Princeton study finds there is great ambiguity about the role of religion in the family and society generally.

117. For a brief but informative summary of the evolution of the concepts of messianic leader and "Son of Man" see Bernard P. Prusak, " 'The Son of Man Came Eating and Drinking': An Overview of Christological

Perspectives on the Incarnation" in *Who Do People Say I Am?*, Proceedings of the Theology Institute of Villanova University, 1980, pp. 22-32.

118. Dwight D. Eisenhower, quoted in Will Herberg, *Protestant, Catholic, Jew* (New York: Anchor Books, 1960), p. 84.

119. The connection between God and country in its American context has been analyzed as "Civil Religion." See Robert Bellah and Phillip E. Hammond, *Varieties of Civil Religion* (San Francisco: Harper & Row, 1980). For a connection between God and the economy see Jeremy Rifkin, with Ted Howard, *The Emerging Order: God in the Age of Scarcity* (New York: Ballantine Books, 1979), pp. X- XVI.

120. The "Death of God" theologians in recent decades exaggerated the social role of Jesus when they defined him exclusively as "the man for others," but the best insights of theology and psychology attest to the impossibility of an authentic religious experience within the Christian tradition which is unconcerned about the needs of others. Langdon Gilkey notes: "Given an ultimate security in God's love, and an ultimate meaning to his own small life in God's eternal purposes, a man can forget his own welfare and for the first time look at his neighbor free from the gropings of self-concern." See his *Shantung Compound* (New York: Harper & Row, 1966), p. 234.

121. Shusaku Endo, trans. Richard A. Schuchert, *A Life of Jesus* (New York: Paulist, 1978), p. 52. This modest work by a Japanese Catholic beautifully conveys both the simplicity and power of the person of Jesus. Intriguing reflections on the deeper and more subtle meaning of Jesus' message are found in Jacob Needleman, *Lost Christianity* (New York: Bantam Books, 1982).

122. Endo, *op. cit.*, pp. 53-54.

123. "Theodicy" is a system of philosophical reflection that seeks to understand how divine justice and love can be aligned with the experience of evil and suffering. The monotheistic religions, for whom this is of central concern, have wrestled with this seeming contradiction in various ways. The Book of Job in the Jewish scriptures is a classic theodicy. It should be

recalled that the Buddha likely found any satisfactory integration so improbable that he explicitly excluded God from his own myth.

124. The Roman authorities were generally tolerant of the myriad religious beliefs that flourished throughout the Empire and which gradually gained devotees within their own walls. Rome was a marketplace of foreign and domestic deities. The Christians were originally viewed as one more Jewish sect, albeit with a rather bizarre doctrine. Persecution flared up for a number of complex political, military and ideological reasons.

125. The offensiveness of the Cross for devout Buddhists reflects the accuracy of Paul's insight (1 Corinthians 1:23). See Dom Aelred Graham, *The End of Religion* (New York: Harvest, 1971), p. 164. Violent death confirms bad karma. For an understanding of the connection between the cross and self-awareness from a Buddhist and Christian perspective see John B. Cobb, Jr., *Beyond Dialogue: Toward a Mutual Transformation of Christainity and Buddhism* (Philadelphia: Fortress Press, 1982), pp. 81-6.

126. For a useful overview of Christian theological reflection, with pertinent references on the Resurrection, the interested reader is referred to William P. Loewe, "The Appearances of the Risen Lord: Faith, Fact and Objectivity," *Horizons,* Vol. 6, no. 2. (Fall, 1979), pp. 177-192.

127. Endo, *op. cit.,* p. 176. The author deals with this central belief of Christianity in a clear and readable fashion for both believer and skeptic. See his chapter "The Question," pp. 156-179.

128. David Tracy, *Blessed Rage for Order* (New York: Seabury Press, 1979), p. 220. The resurrection of Jesus is seen to be a revelation about the very nature of human destiny and our orientation to an existence beyond human comprehension. For example, John S. Dunne, *op. cit.,* p. 214.

129. A 17th century legend had James visit Spain before his martydom and certain traditions claim that Thomas went to Persia (Iran) and India. There are no facts to substantiate these stories, but Rome as the burial site for Peter and Paul is accepted by many historians.

130. Schillebeeckx, *op. cit.,* pp. 47-48. *Shalom* is the Hebrew word for "peace" and has the same root as the Arabic word *salaam* which is the basis for the meaning of Islam.

131. There are indications that Christianity was seen to be the religion of the lower classes for centuries and was deemed to be too democratic by the nobility. The story of Victorinus is instructive here. It is recorded in *The Confessions of St. Augustine,* trans. R.S. Pine-Coffin (New York: Penguin Books, 1980), pp. 159-61.

132. When Rome fell in 410 A.D. to the invading Visigoths, many Christians believed the final days were upon them, so closely did they align the Roman Empire with the future of the Christian religion. It was to categorically reject any essential connection between the eternal Mystical Body and ephemeral nations that Augustine wrote his *City of God.* His emphasis on the primacy of Church over State had significant political and theological results throughout the Middle Ages. The legacy of "theological imperialism" resulting from Constantine's embrace of Christianity is examined by Charles S. McCoy, *When Gods Change* (Nashville: Abingdon Press, 1980), pp. 108-236.

133. Monika K. Hellwig, *Jesus, the Compassion of God* (Wilmington, DE: Michael Glazier, 1983), especially pp. 75-123.

134. A Christian theodicy is grounded in faith in Jesus as the Crucified Risen One. Whatever explanations are put forward to explain suffering within a theistic religion, they all presuppose the prior experience of a purposive and loving God. "A God who is active and available in the midst of every crisis and present in every tragedy is a God who can change the world. The uncertainty is not whether God is with us and able to overcome our suffering, but whether we will join God in the struggle." Howard R. Burkle, *God, Suffering and Belief* (Nashville: Abingdon Press, 1977), p. 121. For an insight into the intrinsic connection between the death of Jesus and the call for social justice, see Edward Schillebeeckx, trans. John Bowden, *Christ, the Experience of Jesus as Lord* (New York: Seabury Press, 1980), pp. 790-846.

Chapter 9—Muhammed: The Myth of the Book

135. Many general history texts used in American classrooms deal with Muslim history almost exclusively in terms of military episodes (*e.g.,* Moorish excursions into France, the Ottomans' seige of Vienna and their

capture of Constantinople, the American forays against the Barbary pirates, *etc.*) and pay little attention to the cultural and religious dislocation thrust upon the Muslim lands by European imperialism in the nineteenth and twentieth centuries. For two very different reactions to this disruptive pattern, see Clifford Geertz, *Islam Observed: Religious Development in Morocco and Indonesia* (Chicago: Phoenix, 1971). Apart from a fortuitous exposure to a specialized course, most college graduates are likely unaware of what Damascus, Baghdad, Cairo, Fez, Toledo or Cordova contributed to world civilization. The names of Ferdawsi, Avicenna and Averroes would be even more obscure, but an educated European of the High Middle Ages would have recognized their genius. The point to be made is that history in the West has tended to be history of the West with entire advanced civilizations relegated to little more than a backdrop against which to trumpet European and American expansion. To be ignorant of this lopsided editing is to be incapable of intelligently reading your daily newspaper and of understanding how and why the East views the West as it does.

136. This chapter will attempt to clarify the implications of this seeming paradox. Muslims, especially the Arab peoples, are the heirs of a vanished Golden Age (roughly from the seventh to the twelfth centuries) and this awareness serves to not only sustain but to frustrate them. Americans have known "Empire" for less than a century, but it is instructive for us to observe the defensiveness aroused by the economic success of Germany and Japan, by the marketing sophistication of the OPEC bloc and by the refusal of our European allies to routinely support our foreign policy decisions in various parts of the world. We may have some incipient sympathy for Arab sensitivities if we reflect on the difficulty the average American has in adjusting to a world that increasingly refuses to define reality in simple pro-American and pro-Soviet polarities. History teaches one inexorable lesson: nations, like individuals, must adjust to their inevitable replacement by others who are younger and more energetic. The Arab Muslim world has experienced this phenomenon but has accepted it with no greater ease than Americans are apt to.

137. For an excellent presentation of the Arab Muslim understanding of history, the reader is encouraged to read Wilfred Cantwell Smith, *Islam in*

Modern History (Princeton: Princeton University Press, 1977). Of equal importance in assisting the reader to comprehend the often hostile Muslim attitude towards the West is Daniel Pipes, *In the Path of God: Islam and Political Power* (New York: Basic Books, 1983). Pipes' study analyzes the situation country by country and provides credible predictions about the options available to Islam in the modern world.

138. It is estimated by some scholars that as many as 60 percent of Muslims practice some form of Sufism. The word "Sufi" is traced to the Arabic word for "wool" and reflects the influence of Christian monastic and mystical practices. Sufis traditionally trace their origin to Hasan al-Basri who died in 728. Sufism seems to have been a popular reaction to the perceived formalism and fatalism of early Islam. It is interesting that some Muslim scholars make no mention of Sufism when describing Islam to a non-Muslim readership. It is evidently judged to imply a threat to the objective and scriptural expression of the faith. For a clear treatment of Sufism, see Marshall G.S. Hodgson, *The Venture of Islam,* vol. 1, (Chicago: University of Chicago Press, 1974), pp. 392-409. The more curious reader is directed to Margaret Smith, *The Way of the Mystics: The Early Christian Mystics and the Rise of the Sufis* (New York: Oxford University Press, 1978). Also informative is Reynold A. Nicholson, *The Mystics of Islam* (New York: Schocken Books, 1975).

139. Smith, *op. cit.,* is especially clear in treating this critical issue in his chapter "The Arabs: Islamic Crisis."

140. G.H. Jansen, *Militant Islam* (New York: Harper & Row, 1979), p. 17. Iran, after the rule of the Shah, has sought to implement this ideal in creating a total Islamic society. Other Muslim nations like Turkey have adopted a Western model of separation of Church and State. The reader should be aware that many adaptations and compromises of the "pure" Islamic society have created a spectrum of political arrangements in the

Muslim world. It remains to be seen whether the forces of modernity will eventually subvert any realistic hope for reimplementing such a vision that served the Muslim world for centuries, at least in certain places. See Pipes, *op. cit.*, pp. 29-69.

141. It is likely that Muhammed learned at least the rudimentary beliefs of the Jewish tradition from the large Jewish clans living in Medina, the city to which he emigrated in 622 A.D. The knowledge that Abraham preceded both Judaism and Christianity may have helped Muhammed to formulate his claim that Abraham and he were the first and last recipients of divine revelation. See Maxime Rodinson, trans. Anne Carter, *Muhammed* (New York: Pantheon Books, 1980), pp. 185-88.

142. Quoted in Rodinson, *op. cit.*, p. 8.

143. The reader is reminded that the kind of facts that an historian seeks is often lacking in the lives of Buddha, Jesus and Muhammed. This does not mean that we are ignorant of these men, but only that biographies in the modern sense of a portrait of detailed and completely verifiable data are not possible. Partisans or opponents of major figures often color a perspective, but the cautious analysis of pious legends and stories will often yield important kernels of truth.

144. The compilation of the *hadith* is a complex study for the general reader. Generally *hadith* is seen to supplement the Koran in legal matters and the consensus of the community is accepted as guaranteeing a traditional saying ascribed to Muhammed. Needless to say, such consensus is often difficult to attain. See Rudi Paret, "Revelation and Tradition in Islam" in Annemarie Schimmel and Ahdoldjavad Falaturi, eds., *We Believe in One God* (New York: Seabury Press, 1979) for a brief treatment of the challenge to modern Islamic scholars relative to *hadith*.

145. The Jew and the Christian are used to a critical exegesis of their sacred texts and major personages, a reflection, perhaps, of trends common in Western scholarship since the Enlightenment. Whether the "average" believer is any more sophisticated in this regard than the "average" Muslim is debatable. A sensitive presentation of Islamic devotion to

Muhammed is given by Annemarie Schimmel in Schimmel and Falaturi, eds., *op. cit.,* pp. 35-61.

146. Rodinson, *op. cit.,* p. 64. The Koran refers to Jews and Christians as the "People of the Book," an honorary designation. Ironically, however, Islam frequently associates Christians and Jews with the unbeliever (*kafir*). See Peter Antes' "Relations with Unbelievers in Islamic Theology," in Schimmel and Falaturi, eds., *op. cit.,* pp. 101-11.

147. The retreat of Gautama into the forest and of Jesus into the desert preceded their respective missions. The ability to be quiet within oneself is a common factor observed in the lives of each of these three major figures.

148. *The Vision of Piers Plowman,* trans. Henry W. Wells (New York: Sheed & Ward, 1945), p. 206; *The Inferno,* trans. John Ciardi (New York: Mentor Books, 1954), p. 236.

149. Zaka Ullab, an Indian Muslim leader, speaking to a Christian friend. Quoted in Kenneth Cragg and Marston Speight, *Islam From Within* (Belmont, CA: Wadsworth, 1980), p. 11. Muslims insist that the power and sublime beauty of the Koran can never be communicated in any translation. Reading—or better, chanting (Qu'ran = "to recite")—the Koran must be in Arabic if one is to appreciate Ullab's assertion. With that limitation noted, N.J. Dawood's translation (Harmondsworth, England: Penguin, 1979) will be cited in this chapter.

150. The Koran consists of 114 surahs or chapters. The Koran is about the length of the New Testament, but it follows no chronological sequence. The surahs are generally arranged from longest to shortest, creating consternation for the reader used to the thematic and historical patterns of the Old and New Testaments.

151. These were spirit-creatures who lived in the desert and were believed capable of invading human beings. The Koran attests that God created them, along with human beings and angels.

152. Many Muslims hold that Muhammed was illiterate and insist that only Allah's power can account for such an incredible masterpiece. Scholars discount this as pious legend and argue that the caravan trade

overseen by Muhammed would have required basic reading, writing and math skills.

153. Kenneth Cragg, *Muhammed and the Christian* (New York: Orbis Books, 1984), p. 102. Cragg's work is essential reading for the Christian sincerely disposed to learn more about Islam and to ponder possible areas of agreement.

154. The Kaaba stone, likely a large meteorite, then as now stands in the center of the holy city of Mecca. In Muhammed's time this edifice was covered with over three hundred statues dedicated to various gods and goddesses. When he entered Mecca in triumph in 630 A.D. Muhammed destroyed these idols and dedicated it to Allah. Muslims believe that Abraham and his son Ishmael (Genesis 16) shaped the Kaaba stone. This stone remains the most sacred shrine in Islam.

155. The *hijrah* or "emigration" in 622 A.D. marks the beginning of the Islamic calendar. Thus 622 A.D. becomes 1 A.H. ("year of the *hijrah*") and the dividing line between the revelations in Mecca and Medina.

156. Muhammed and his followers had prayed towards Jerusalem and recognized the Jewish sabbath as their holy day. When it became apparent that the Jews of Medina would not acquiesce in his claim that Islam superseded all other revelations, Muhammed instructed his followers to pray in the direction of Mecca. The Muslim house of prayer, the mosque, is said to be modeled on Muhammed's house in Medina. Friday became the holy day of Islam, distinct from the Jewish sabbath and the Christian Sunday, and devout male Muslims are expected to attend the mosque on this day.

157. The complex patterns of tribal custom, legal obligation and clan psychology prevalent in a seventh century desert society may help explain, if not justify, such atrocities to the modern reader. More problematic even for the very sympathetic scholars, is the fact that such episodes were not seen to be historical aberrations, but rather divinely sanctioned. The student of the Jewish Bible is aware of similar horrors, ostensibly approved by God, committed by the ancient Israelites. See especially Deuteronomy and Joshua. Christians must also recognize the distorted religious impulse sustaining the persecution of the Jews, the Inquisition, slavery and

witchcraft trials among a longer list of despicable rationalizations. The employment of *jihad* ("righteous struggle") to combat the enemies of Islam clearly has a basis in the Koran. Its employment, contrary to some contemporary claims, requires approval by the *umma* and is not meant to be a common practice. Some Islamic scholars argue military *jihad* is inapplicable in the modern world.

158. Pipes, *op. cit.,* p. 71.

159. Bernard Lewis contends that population pressures in the Arabian peninsula, rather than religious fervor, accounts for the initial conquests of the Arabs. *The Arabs in History* (New York: Harper Torchbooks, 1967), p. 55.

160. These were non-Muslim peoples, usually Christians or Jews, who lived within territory ruled by Muslims. They were permitted to practice their religion but were subjected to overt social stigmas (*e.g.*, they could not hold government offices, ride horses, *etc.*) The *dhimmis* were also taxed at a higher rate than Muslims so it was to their advantage to discourage *dhimmis* from converting to Islam and thus reducing tax revenues for the State. This is a paradox, of course, since Islam envisions its mission as the call to convert all humankind to Allah's message.

161. Thomas W. Lippman, *Understanding Islam* (New York: Mentor Books, 1982), pp. 8-11. See, e.g., Surah 4:54-59.

162. If he prays in a mosque, the Muslim knows the location of Mecca by the *mihrah,* a directional niche in the wall. Mosque attendance is required only on Friday at midday and on two major religious holidays, and then only for males. The prayer leader is not a priest but an *iman,* a man learned in the Koran. His role would be the same as a rabbi in Judaism. In Muhammed's lifetime prayer was required only thrice daily.

163. A mosque has no pews or reserved seating for dignitaries. All are equal before Allah. This fact had a tremendous impact on the American Black Muslim, Malcolm X, leading him to rethink his hostility towards white persons when he returned from Mecca. See the *Autobiography of Malcolm X* (New York: Grove, 1964).

164. It is probable that Muhammed knew of the Jewish practice of tithing, giving one-tenth of one's produce or income to the community for the needy. Early Christianity also supported this practice and some Christian Churches still require it.

165. 622 A.D. is thus 1 A.H. (year of the *hegira*) when Muhammed fled Mecca for Medina. In the course of a century the Islamic calendar diverges from the Gregorian calendar by about two years.

166. Both Judaism and Christianity prescribe ascetical practices to lessen material attachments and to increase spiritual awareness. Ideally, the Muslim is made conscious of the poor who are hungry and in need.

167. For the specific rituals performed by the faithful on *haji*, the reader is referred to Lippman, *op. cit.*, pp. 22-30. The focus of devotion is on the Kaaba, which Muslims believe was constructed by Abraham and his first-born son, Ishmael. See Genesis 21 for the Jewish version of this incident.

168. Non-Muslims are forbidden to enter Mecca under pain of death, but the rites are now televised to Muslim countries with English commentary provided. Saudi Arabia also provides color slides of the rituals to interested buyers.

169. In popular Muslim piety the man Muhammed has often been raised to the level of near-deity. See Rodinson, *op. cit.*, pp. 293-313 for some intriguing examples of this process.

170. The status of women in Islam often generates a very defensive response from Muslim scholars, yet the fact remains that women are to be sequestered because they are "dangerous." See Pipes, *op. cit.*, pp. 176-182 for a useful overview of male-female relations in Islam. The reader is reminded, however, that nearly every religious system is sexist. Christianity, *e.g.*, has long history of distorting the female image. Judaism, Buddhism, Hinduism, *etc.* are also guilty of such practices. See Denise Carmody, *Women and World Religions* (Nashville: Abingdon Press, 1979), pp. 49-50.

Chapter 10—Concluding Remarks

171. See Peter Berger, *The Heretical Imperative* (Garden City, NJ: Anchor Books, 1980), pp. 1-29 for some interesting implications for religion as "modernity" becomes the universal human experience.

172. This phrase is used by the German sociologist of religion, Max Weber, to refer to those individuals like the Buddha, Jesus and Muhammed, to name only three, who claimed to have had an intense, personal experience of ultimate reality. See his *The Sociology of Religion,* trans. Ephraim Fischoff (Boston: Beacon Press, 1964), pp. 151-65.

173. The term "fundamentalist" refers to an individual who believes that his or her religious tradition is the exclusive means of salvation or truth. All other beliefs are simply in error and are not to be accorded respect. When fundamentalism has a scriptural foundation (*i.e.,* Judaism, Christianity, Islam, and certain expressions of Hinduism, *etc.*), believers hold that each word is literally free of error.

174. A problem for any reflective believer in one myth rather than in another is how to integrate commitment (*e.g.,* to Jesus or the Koran) with tolerance and respect for other alternatives in a religiously (and irreligiously) diversified world. This question has attracted the attention of many thinkers in all traditions. See for example, Donald G. Dawe and John B. Carmen, ed., *Christian Faith in a Religiously Plural World* (New York: Orbis Books, 1978); Wilfred Cantwell Smith, *Religious Diversity* (New York: Crossroad, 1982); and Paul F. Knitter, *No Other Name?* (New York: Orbis Books, 1985). The serious student of this topic will find presented in these books the whole spectrum of theological positions.

175. Berger, *op. cit.,* p. 165-72. This phrase neatly integrates Christian commitment with openness to seeking truth from whatever source.